50 Premium Restaurant Dessert Recipes for Home

By: Kelly Johnson

Table of Contents

- Lemon Tart with Raspberry Coulis
- Chocolate Fondant with Vanilla Ice Cream
- Pistachio Crème Brûlée
- Grand Marnier Soufflé
- Tiramisu with Espresso Soaked Ladyfingers
- Raspberry Lemonade Sorbet
- Basil and Strawberry Shortcake
- Caramelized Banana Pudding with Salted Caramel Sauce
- Matcha Green Tea Cheesecake
- Hazelnut Praline Mousse
- White Chocolate and Lavender Panna Cotta
- Almond and Cherry Clafoutis
- Dark Chocolate and Sea Salt Tart
- Passion Fruit and Mango Panna Cotta
- Bourbon Pecan Pie with Bourbon Caramel Sauce
- Coconut and Lime Rice Pudding
- Fig and Walnut Tart with Honey Glaze
- Mascarpone and Berry Parfait
- Pomegranate and Mint Granita
- Raspberry Macarons with Lemon Filling
- Spiced Apple Compote with Cinnamon Gelato
- Chocolate Lava Cake with Raspberry Coulis
- Caramelized Pear and Almond Tart
- Vanilla Bean Crème Brûlée with Fresh Berries
- Mocha Tiramisu with Coffee Soaked Cake
- Orange Blossom and Honey Cheesecake
- Gingerbread Panna Cotta with Cardamom Syrup
- Salted Caramel Chocolate Cheesecake
- Pear and Almond Cake with Amaretto Glaze
- Mango Sticky Rice with Coconut Sauce
- Cherry Clafoutis with Almond Cream
- Lime and Coconut Mousse with Pineapple Salsa

- Raspberry and Rosewater Panna Cotta
- Blackberry and Sage Tart
- Chai Spiced Poached Pears
- Tiramisu Cheesecake with Coffee Cream
- White Chocolate and Passion Fruit Mousse
- Pistachio and Rosewater Baklava
- Espresso Bean Chocolate Truffles
- Pineapple Upside-Down Cake with Rum Glaze
- Chocolaty Chestnut Mousse Cake
- Apple Cinnamon Bread Pudding with Bourbon Sauce
- Maple Pecan Pie with Bourbon Cream
- Cardamom and Saffron Rice Pudding
- Black Sesame and Ginger Ice Cream
- Mango Coconut Chia Pudding
- Lavender Honey Cheesecake
- Plum and Almond Frangipane Tart
- Spiced Chocolate Soufflé with Vanilla Cream
- Balsamic Strawberry and Basil Sorbet

Lemon Tart with Raspberry Coulis

Ingredients:

For the Tart Crust:

- 1 1/4 cups all-purpose flour
- 1/4 cup granulated sugar
- 1/2 cup unsalted butter, cold and cut into small pieces
- 1/4 teaspoon salt
- 1 large egg yolk
- 2 tablespoons ice water (as needed)

For the Lemon Filling:

- 1 cup granulated sugar
- 1/2 cup freshly squeezed lemon juice (about 3 lemons)
- 2 large eggs
- 1 large egg yolk
- 1/2 cup heavy cream
- 2 tablespoons unsalted butter

Instructions:

1. **Prepare the Crust:**
    - In a food processor, combine the flour, sugar, and salt. Add the cold butter and pulse until the mixture resembles coarse crumbs.
    - Add the egg yolk and pulse. Gradually add the ice water until the dough begins to come together. Be careful not to overwork it.
    - Form the dough into a disc, wrap in plastic wrap, and chill in the refrigerator for at least 30 minutes.
2. **Preheat Oven:**
    - Preheat your oven to 375°F (190°C).
3. **Roll Out and Bake the Crust:**
    - On a lightly floured surface, roll out the dough to fit a 9-inch tart pan. Gently press the dough into the pan and trim any excess.
    - Line the dough with parchment paper and fill with pie weights or dried beans. Bake for 15 minutes, then remove the parchment and weights and bake for an additional 5 minutes until golden. Let cool.
4. **Make the Lemon Filling:**
    - In a medium saucepan, combine the sugar and lemon juice. Heat over medium heat until the sugar dissolves.
    - In a bowl, whisk together the eggs and egg yolk. Gradually whisk in the warm lemon mixture.

- Return the mixture to the saucepan and cook over medium heat, stirring constantly, until it thickens and reaches 170°F (77°C) on a thermometer. Remove from heat and stir in the butter until smooth.
- Pour the filling into the cooled tart crust and smooth the top. Bake for 15-20 minutes until the filling is set. Let cool to room temperature.

Raspberry Coulis

Ingredients:

- 1 cup fresh or frozen raspberries
- 1/4 cup granulated sugar
- 1 tablespoon lemon juice

Instructions:

1. **Make the Coulis:**
    - In a medium saucepan, combine raspberries, sugar, and lemon juice. Cook over medium heat, stirring occasionally, until the raspberries break down and the mixture is slightly thickened (about 5-7 minutes).
    - Strain the mixture through a fine-mesh sieve to remove seeds and solids, pressing with a spoon to extract as much liquid as possible.
    - Allow the coulis to cool to room temperature.

To Serve:

- Slice the cooled lemon tart and drizzle with raspberry coulis. You can also garnish with fresh raspberries or mint leaves if desired.

Enjoy your elegant dessert!

Chocolate Fondant with Vanilla Ice Cream

Ingredients:

- 1/2 cup (115g) unsalted butter, plus extra for greasing
- 4 oz (115g) high-quality dark chocolate (70% cocoa), chopped
- 1 cup (125g) powdered sugar
- 2 large eggs
- 2 large egg yolks
- 1 teaspoon vanilla extract
- 1/2 cup (65g) all-purpose flour
- Pinch of salt

Instructions:

1. **Prepare Ramekins:**
   - Preheat your oven to 425°F (220°C).
   - Butter 4 ramekins (6 oz or 180ml each) and dust with cocoa powder, tapping out any excess.
2. **Make the Fondant Batter:**
   - In a medium heatproof bowl, melt the butter and chocolate together over a pot of simmering water (double boiler method), stirring until smooth. Remove from heat.
   - Stir in the powdered sugar until well combined.
   - Add the eggs and egg yolks, mixing thoroughly.
   - Stir in the vanilla extract.
   - Gently fold in the flour and salt until just combined.
3. **Bake:**
   - Divide the batter evenly among the prepared ramekins.
   - Bake for 10-12 minutes, until the edges are set but the centers are still soft and slightly jiggly.
4. **Serve:**
   - Let the fondants cool in the ramekins for 1 minute. Carefully run a knife around the edges and invert them onto plates.
   - Serve immediately with a scoop of vanilla ice cream.

Vanilla Ice Cream

Ingredients:

- 2 cups (500ml) heavy cream
- 1 cup (250ml) whole milk
- 3/4 cup (150g) granulated sugar
- 1 tablespoon vanilla extract
- 4 large egg yolks

Instructions:

1. **Prepare the Ice Cream Base:**
    - In a saucepan, heat the milk and cream over medium heat until it begins to steam. Do not let it boil.
    - In a bowl, whisk the egg yolks and sugar until pale and slightly thickened.
    - Gradually pour the hot milk mixture into the egg yolks, whisking constantly to temper the yolks.
    - Return the mixture to the saucepan and cook over medium heat, stirring constantly with a wooden spoon, until it thickens and coats the back of the spoon (about 170°F or 77°C).
2. **Chill and Churn:**
    - Remove from heat and stir in the vanilla extract.
    - Transfer the custard to a bowl and let it cool to room temperature, then refrigerate until thoroughly chilled (at least 4 hours or overnight).
    - Churn the custard in an ice cream maker according to the manufacturer's instructions until it reaches a soft-serve consistency.
    - Transfer to an airtight container and freeze until firm.

To Serve:

- Plate the chocolate fondants and top with a generous scoop of homemade vanilla ice cream.
- Optionally, you can garnish with fresh berries, a sprinkle of powdered sugar, or a drizzle of chocolate sauce.

Enjoy your rich and decadent dessert!

Pistachio Crème Brûlée

Ingredients:

For the Pistachio Crème Brûlée:

- 2 cups (500ml) heavy cream
- 1/2 cup (120ml) whole milk
- 1/2 cup (100g) granulated sugar
- 1/2 cup (60g) unsalted pistachios, shelled and finely ground
- 5 large egg yolks
- 1 teaspoon vanilla extract
- 1/4 teaspoon almond extract (optional, for enhanced flavor)

For the Caramelized Sugar Topping:

- 1/4 cup (50g) granulated sugar

Instructions:

1. **Preheat Oven:**
    - Preheat your oven to 325°F (160°C).
2. **Prepare the Cream Mixture:**
    - In a medium saucepan, combine the heavy cream, milk, and granulated sugar. Heat over medium heat until it just begins to simmer, stirring occasionally.
    - Remove from heat and stir in the finely ground pistachios. Let the mixture steep for 10-15 minutes to infuse the pistachio flavor. Strain through a fine-mesh sieve to remove the pistachio pieces.
3. **Prepare the Custard Base:**
    - In a large bowl, whisk the egg yolks until they become pale and slightly thickened.
    - Gradually add the warm cream mixture to the egg yolks, whisking constantly to temper the yolks and prevent curdling.
    - Stir in the vanilla extract and almond extract, if using.
4. **Bake the Crème Brûlée:**
    - Divide the custard mixture evenly among 4 to 6 ramekins (depending on size).
    - Place the ramekins in a baking dish. Pour hot water into the baking dish until it reaches halfway up the sides of the ramekins to create a water bath.
    - Bake for 35-40 minutes, or until the edges are set but the centers are still slightly jiggly. The custards should be just set but still soft in the middle.
    - Remove from the oven and let the ramekins cool in the water bath for about 30 minutes. Then remove from the water bath and refrigerate for at least 2 hours, or overnight.
5. **Caramelize the Sugar:**

- Just before serving, sprinkle a thin, even layer of granulated sugar over the top of each custard.
- Use a kitchen torch to caramelize the sugar until it forms a golden, crispy crust. Move the torch in a circular motion to ensure even caramelization. If you don't have a torch, you can place the ramekins under a broiler for 1-2 minutes, but watch carefully to prevent burning.

6. **Serve:**
    - Allow the crème brûlée to sit for a few minutes after caramelizing to let the sugar harden before serving.

Tips:

- **Pistachio Quality:** For the best flavor, use high-quality, unsalted pistachios.
- **Straining:** Strain the cream mixture well to ensure a smooth custard.
- **Torch:** A kitchen torch is ideal for caramelizing the sugar. If using a broiler, keep a close eye to avoid burning.

Enjoy your elegant and creamy Pistachio Crème Brûlée!

Grand Marnier Soufflé

Ingredients:

For the Soufflé Base:

- 2 tablespoons unsalted butter, plus extra for greasing
- 1/2 cup granulated sugar (for coating)
- 1/2 cup whole milk
- 1/4 cup all-purpose flour
- 1/4 teaspoon salt
- 3 large egg yolks
- 2 tablespoons Grand Marnier (or other orange liqueur)
- 1 teaspoon vanilla extract

For the Meringue:

- 3 large egg whites
- 1/4 teaspoon cream of tartar
- 1/4 cup granulated sugar

For the Garnish:

- Powdered sugar, for dusting (optional)

Instructions:

1. **Prepare the Ramekins:**
    - Preheat your oven to 375°F (190°C).
    - Generously butter four 6-ounce (180ml) ramekins, making sure to coat the sides thoroughly. Sprinkle granulated sugar inside the ramekins, tapping out any excess. This helps the soufflé rise evenly.
2. **Make the Soufflé Base:**
    - In a medium saucepan, melt 2 tablespoons of butter over medium heat. Add the flour and salt, and cook, stirring constantly, for 2-3 minutes to make a roux (a thick paste).
    - Gradually whisk in the milk, and cook until the mixture thickens and becomes smooth (about 2-3 minutes).
    - Remove from heat and stir in the egg yolks, one at a time, until fully incorporated.
    - Mix in the Grand Marnier and vanilla extract. Allow the mixture to cool to room temperature.
3. **Prepare the Meringue:**
    - In a clean, dry mixing bowl, beat the egg whites and cream of tartar with an electric mixer on medium speed until soft peaks form.

- Gradually add the granulated sugar, continuing to beat until stiff, glossy peaks form.
4. **Fold the Meringue into the Soufflé Base:**
    - Gently fold a small portion of the meringue into the soufflé base to lighten it. Then fold in the remaining meringue carefully, using a spatula to avoid deflating the mixture. Be gentle to maintain the airy texture.
5. **Fill the Ramekins and Bake:**
    - Spoon the soufflé mixture into the prepared ramekins, filling them to just below the rim. Run your finger around the edge of each ramekin to help the soufflés rise evenly.
    - Place the ramekins on a baking sheet and bake for 12-15 minutes, or until the soufflés have risen and are golden brown on top. Avoid opening the oven door during baking.
6. **Serve:**
    - Dust with powdered sugar if desired, and serve immediately. Soufflés are best enjoyed straight from the oven while they are still puffed and warm.

Tips:

- **Room Temperature Ingredients:** Make sure your ingredients are at room temperature for the best results.
- **Beating Egg Whites:** Ensure your mixing bowl and beaters are clean and free of grease to achieve the best meringue.
- **Serving:** Soufflés can deflate quickly, so serve them immediately after baking for the best presentation.

Enjoy your elegant and airy Grand Marnier Soufflé!

Tiramisu with Espresso Soaked Ladyfingers

Ingredients:

For the Espresso Mixture:

- 1 cup (240ml) strong brewed espresso, cooled
- 1/4 cup (60ml) coffee liqueur (such as Kahlúa) or Marsala wine (optional)

For the Mascarpone Mixture:

- 1 cup (240ml) heavy cream
- 8 oz (225g) mascarpone cheese, room temperature
- 1/2 cup (100g) granulated sugar
- 1 teaspoon vanilla extract
- 3 large egg yolks

For the Assembly:

- 24-30 ladyfingers (savoiardi), depending on size
- Unsweetened cocoa powder, for dusting
- Dark chocolate shavings or cocoa powder, for garnish (optional)

Instructions:

1. **Prepare the Espresso Mixture:**
   - In a shallow dish, combine the cooled espresso with coffee liqueur or Marsala wine, if using. Set aside.
2. **Prepare the Mascarpone Mixture:**
   - In a medium bowl, whisk the egg yolks and granulated sugar together until pale and slightly thickened.
   - In a saucepan, heat a few inches of water to simmer (double boiler method). Place the bowl with egg yolks and sugar over the simmering water (make sure the bottom of the bowl does not touch the water) and whisk constantly until the mixture is warm and slightly thickened (about 2-3 minutes). Remove from heat and allow to cool slightly.
   - In a large mixing bowl, beat the heavy cream until stiff peaks form.
   - Gently fold the mascarpone cheese and vanilla extract into the egg yolk mixture until smooth.
   - Carefully fold the whipped cream into the mascarpone mixture until well combined and smooth.
3. **Assemble the Tiramisu:**
   - Quickly dip each ladyfinger into the espresso mixture, making sure not to soak them. They should be coated but not overly soggy.

- Arrange a layer of dipped ladyfingers in the bottom of a 9x13-inch (23x33 cm) dish or individual serving glasses.
- Spread half of the mascarpone mixture over the layer of ladyfingers.
- Add another layer of dipped ladyfingers on top of the mascarpone mixture.
- Spread the remaining mascarpone mixture evenly over the top layer of ladyfingers.

4. **Chill and Serve:**
    - Cover and refrigerate the tiramisu for at least 4 hours, or preferably overnight, to allow the flavors to meld and the dessert to set.
    - Before serving, dust the top with unsweetened cocoa powder and garnish with dark chocolate shavings or additional cocoa powder if desired.

Tips:

- **Espresso Strength:** Use strong brewed espresso for a robust coffee flavor. If you don't have an espresso machine, you can use strong coffee.
- **Ladyfingers:** Be quick when dipping the ladyfingers to avoid them becoming too soggy.
- **Chilling Time:** The longer the tiramisu chills, the better the flavors will develop.

Enjoy your indulgent and creamy tiramisu with espresso-soaked ladyfingers!

Raspberry Lemonade Sorbet

Ingredients:

- 2 cups (250g) fresh or frozen raspberries
- 1 cup (200g) granulated sugar
- 1 cup (240ml) freshly squeezed lemon juice (about 4-6 lemons)
- 1 cup (240ml) water
- 1 teaspoon lemon zest (optional, for added flavor)
- Mint leaves, for garnish (optional)

Instructions:

1. **Prepare the Raspberry Puree:**
   - In a blender or food processor, blend the raspberries until smooth.
   - Strain the raspberry puree through a fine-mesh sieve into a bowl, pressing down with a spatula to extract as much liquid as possible. Discard the seeds.
2. **Make the Simple Syrup:**
   - In a medium saucepan, combine the water and granulated sugar.
   - Heat over medium heat, stirring occasionally, until the sugar is completely dissolved. Allow the syrup to cool to room temperature.
3. **Combine Ingredients:**
   - Stir the raspberry puree and lemon juice into the cooled simple syrup.
   - If using, mix in the lemon zest for extra lemon flavor.
4. **Churn the Sorbet:**
   - Pour the mixture into an ice cream maker and churn according to the manufacturer's instructions until it reaches a smooth, slushy consistency (usually about 20-30 minutes).
5. **Freeze and Serve:**
   - Transfer the churned sorbet to an airtight container and freeze for at least 2 hours to firm up.
   - Before serving, let the sorbet sit at room temperature for a few minutes to soften slightly, then scoop into bowls or glasses.
   - Garnish with fresh mint leaves, if desired.

Tips:

- **Taste Test:** Before freezing, taste the mixture and adjust the sweetness if needed. If it's too tart, you can add a bit more sugar.
- **No Ice Cream Maker:** If you don't have an ice cream maker, pour the mixture into a shallow dish and freeze. Every 30 minutes, stir with a fork to break up ice crystals until the sorbet is frozen and fluffy.

Enjoy your delightful and tangy Raspberry Lemonade Sorbet!

Basil and Strawberry Shortcake

Ingredients:

For the Shortcakes:

- 2 cups (250g) all-purpose flour
- 1/4 cup (50g) granulated sugar
- 1 tablespoon baking powder
- 1/2 teaspoon salt
- 1/2 cup (115g) unsalted butter, cold and cut into small pieces
- 2/3 cup (160ml) heavy cream
- 1 large egg
- 1 teaspoon vanilla extract

For the Basil Strawberry Filling:

- 4 cups (500g) fresh strawberries, hulled and sliced
- 1/4 cup (50g) granulated sugar (adjust based on strawberry sweetness)
- 1/4 cup (60ml) fresh lemon juice
- 1/4 cup (60ml) finely chopped fresh basil leaves

For the Whipped Cream:

- 1 cup (240ml) heavy cream
- 2 tablespoons powdered sugar
- 1/2 teaspoon vanilla extract

Instructions:

1. **Prepare the Shortcakes:**
    - Preheat your oven to 425°F (220°C).
    - In a large bowl, whisk together the flour, sugar, baking powder, and salt.
    - Cut in the cold butter using a pastry cutter or your fingers until the mixture resembles coarse crumbs.
    - In a separate bowl, whisk together the heavy cream, egg, and vanilla extract.
    - Add the wet ingredients to the dry ingredients and mix until just combined. Do not overmix.
    - Turn the dough out onto a lightly floured surface and gently knead a few times. Pat the dough to a 1-inch thickness.
    - Cut out shortcakes using a round cutter (about 2-3 inches in diameter) and place them on a baking sheet lined with parchment paper.
    - Bake for 12-15 minutes, or until the shortcakes are golden brown. Let cool on a wire rack.
2. **Prepare the Basil Strawberry Filling:**

- In a large bowl, combine the sliced strawberries, sugar, lemon juice, and chopped basil.
    - Gently toss to coat the strawberries with the sugar and basil. Let sit for at least 30 minutes to allow the flavors to meld and the strawberries to release their juices.
3. **Prepare the Whipped Cream:**
    - In a chilled mixing bowl, beat the heavy cream, powdered sugar, and vanilla extract with an electric mixer until stiff peaks form.
4. **Assemble the Shortcakes:**
    - Split the cooled shortcakes in half horizontally.
    - Spoon a generous amount of the basil strawberry filling onto the bottom half of each shortcake.
    - Top with a dollop of whipped cream.
    - Place the top half of the shortcake over the cream and garnish with additional strawberries and basil if desired.

Tips:

- **Basil Flavor:** For a more pronounced basil flavor, you can let the basil sit with the strawberries for a bit longer before serving.
- **Shortcake Variations:** You can also add a bit of lemon zest to the shortcake dough for an extra layer of flavor.
- **Whipped Cream:** Make sure your mixing bowl and beaters are cold to achieve the best results with the whipped cream.

Enjoy your delightful and aromatic Basil and Strawberry Shortcake!

Caramelized Banana Pudding with Salted Caramel Sauce

Ingredients:

For the Caramelized Bananas:

- 4 ripe bananas, sliced
- 1/4 cup (50g) granulated sugar
- 1 tablespoon unsalted butter

For the Banana Pudding:

- 2 cups (480ml) whole milk
- 1/2 cup (100g) granulated sugar
- 1/4 cup (30g) cornstarch
- 1/4 teaspoon salt
- 4 large egg yolks
- 1 teaspoon vanilla extract
- 1/2 cup (120ml) heavy cream

For the Salted Caramel Sauce:

- 1 cup (200g) granulated sugar
- 6 tablespoons unsalted butter, cut into pieces
- 1/2 cup (120ml) heavy cream
- 1/2 teaspoon sea salt (or to taste)

Instructions:

1. **Prepare the Caramelized Bananas:**
    - In a large skillet, melt the butter over medium heat.
    - Add the sugar and stir until it starts to dissolve and bubble.
    - Add the banana slices and cook for about 2-3 minutes on each side, or until they are golden brown and caramelized. Remove from heat and set aside.
2. **Make the Banana Pudding:**
    - In a medium saucepan, combine the milk, sugar, cornstarch, and salt. Whisk until smooth.
    - Cook over medium heat, whisking constantly, until the mixture comes to a boil and thickens (about 5-7 minutes).
    - In a separate bowl, lightly whisk the egg yolks.
    - Gradually add a few spoonfuls of the hot milk mixture to the egg yolks, whisking constantly to temper the yolks.
    - Pour the egg yolk mixture back into the saucepan with the remaining milk mixture.
    - Continue to cook, whisking constantly, until the pudding thickens further (about 2-3 minutes). Remove from heat.

- Stir in the vanilla extract and let the pudding cool for a few minutes.
- Fold in the heavy cream until fully combined and smooth.

3. **Make the Salted Caramel Sauce:**
   - In a medium saucepan over medium heat, melt the sugar, stirring constantly until it turns an amber color.
   - Carefully add the butter (it will bubble vigorously) and stir until melted and combined.
   - Gradually add the heavy cream while stirring continuously. The mixture will bubble up again.
   - Remove from heat and stir in the sea salt. Allow the sauce to cool slightly before using.

4. **Assemble the Dessert:**
   - Spoon a layer of banana pudding into serving glasses or bowls.
   - Top with a layer of caramelized bananas.
   - Repeat layers until you reach the top of the container, finishing with pudding.
   - Drizzle with warm salted caramel sauce just before serving.

Tips:

- **Caramel Temperature:** Be careful when making caramel as it can get very hot. Use a long-handled spoon and avoid touching the hot caramel.
- **Pudding Consistency:** If the pudding becomes too thick after cooling, you can whisk in a little milk to reach your desired consistency.
- **Advance Preparation:** You can make the pudding and caramel sauce ahead of time and refrigerate them separately. Assemble the dessert just before serving for the best texture.

Enjoy your luxurious Caramelized Banana Pudding with Salted Caramel Sauce!

Matcha Green Tea Cheesecake

Ingredients:

For the Crust:

- 1 1/2 cups (150g) graham cracker crumbs
- 1/4 cup (50g) granulated sugar
- 1/2 cup (115g) unsalted butter, melted

For the Cheesecake Filling:

- 4 (8 oz each) packages (900g) cream cheese, softened
- 1 cup (200g) granulated sugar
- 1/4 cup (60ml) sour cream
- 1/4 cup (60ml) heavy cream
- 3 large eggs
- 1 tablespoon matcha green tea powder (preferably culinary grade)
- 1 teaspoon vanilla extract

For the Topping (optional):

- 1/4 cup (60ml) sour cream
- 2 tablespoons granulated sugar
- 1 tablespoon matcha green tea powder

Instructions:

1. **Prepare the Crust:**
    - Preheat your oven to 325°F (160°C).
    - In a medium bowl, combine the graham cracker crumbs, granulated sugar, and melted butter. Mix until the crumbs are evenly coated.
    - Press the mixture firmly into the bottom of a 9-inch (23 cm) springform pan to form an even layer.
    - Bake for 10 minutes, then remove from the oven and let cool.
2. **Prepare the Cheesecake Filling:**
    - In a large mixing bowl, beat the softened cream cheese with an electric mixer until smooth and creamy.
    - Gradually add the granulated sugar, mixing until well combined.
    - Add the sour cream and heavy cream, and beat until smooth.
    - In a small bowl, whisk the matcha powder with a few tablespoons of hot water to make a smooth paste. Add this paste to the cream cheese mixture and beat until well incorporated.
    - Add the eggs, one at a time, mixing on low speed after each addition until just combined. Be careful not to overmix.
    - Stir in the vanilla extract.
3. **Bake the Cheesecake:**
    - Pour the cheesecake filling over the cooled crust in the springform pan.

- Smooth the top with a spatula.
- Bake for 50-60 minutes, or until the edges are set but the center is still slightly jiggly. Turn off the oven and crack the oven door slightly. Let the cheesecake cool in the oven for 1 hour.
- After cooling, remove the cheesecake from the oven and refrigerate for at least 4 hours or overnight to fully set.

4. **Prepare the Topping (optional):**
   - In a small bowl, mix the sour cream, granulated sugar, and matcha powder until smooth.
   - Spread this mixture evenly over the chilled cheesecake.

5. **Serve:**
   - Release and remove the sides of the springform pan.
   - Slice the cheesecake and serve chilled. Garnish with additional matcha powder or fresh berries if desired.

Tips:

- **Matcha Quality:** Use high-quality culinary grade matcha powder for the best flavor and color.
- **Avoid Cracking:** To prevent cracks, avoid overmixing the batter and bake the cheesecake at a lower temperature. A water bath can also help in reducing cracks but is optional.
- **Chilling Time:** Allowing the cheesecake to chill overnight enhances the flavors and helps the texture.

Enjoy your elegant and flavorful Matcha Green Tea Cheesecake!

Hazelnut Praline Mousse

Ingredients:

For the Hazelnut Praline:

- 1 cup (150g) whole hazelnuts, toasted and skinless
- 1/2 cup (100g) granulated sugar
- 2 tablespoons water

For the Mousse:

- 4 oz (115g) dark chocolate, chopped
- 2 tablespoons unsalted butter
- 1/2 cup (120ml) heavy cream
- 3 large egg yolks
- 1/4 cup (50g) granulated sugar
- 1 teaspoon vanilla extract
- 1/2 cup (120ml) heavy cream (for whipping)

For Garnish (optional):

- Chopped hazelnuts
- Whipped cream
- Chocolate shavings

Instructions:

1. **Prepare the Hazelnut Praline:**
    - In a medium saucepan, combine the sugar and water. Cook over medium heat, stirring occasionally, until the sugar dissolves and the mixture comes to a boil.
    - Continue cooking without stirring until the mixture turns a deep amber color (about 8-10 minutes). Be careful not to burn it.
    - Remove from heat and quickly stir in the toasted hazelnuts. Pour the mixture onto a baking sheet lined with parchment paper to cool and harden.
    - Once cooled, break the praline into pieces and blend in a food processor until it forms a coarse paste. Set aside.
2. **Make the Chocolate Base:**
    - In a heatproof bowl, melt the dark chocolate and butter together over a pot of simmering water (double boiler method) or in the microwave in 30-second intervals, stirring until smooth.
    - Let the chocolate mixture cool slightly.
3. **Prepare the Mousse Mixture:**
    - In a medium saucepan, heat 1/2 cup of heavy cream until it just begins to simmer. Remove from heat and gradually whisk into the chocolate mixture.
    - In a separate bowl, whisk together the egg yolks and granulated sugar until thick and pale.

- Gradually add a small amount of the warm chocolate mixture into the egg yolks, whisking constantly to temper the yolks.
- Return the egg yolk mixture to the saucepan and cook over medium heat, whisking constantly, until it reaches 170°F (77°C) and thickens slightly. Do not let it boil.
- Remove from heat and stir in the vanilla extract. Let the mixture cool to room temperature.

4. **Whip the Cream:**
    - In a mixing bowl, beat 1/2 cup of heavy cream until stiff peaks form.
    - Gently fold the whipped cream into the cooled chocolate mixture until well combined.

5. **Assemble the Mousse:**
    - Spoon or pipe the mousse into individual serving glasses or bowls.
    - Chill in the refrigerator for at least 2 hours to set.

6. **Garnish and Serve:**
    - Before serving, garnish with chopped hazelnuts, a dollop of whipped cream, and chocolate shavings if desired.

Tips:

- **Hazelnuts:** Toast hazelnuts in the oven at 350°F (175°C) for about 10 minutes until fragrant, then rub in a kitchen towel to remove skins.
- **Praline:** Be cautious when working with hot caramel, as it can burn.
- **Mousse Consistency:** Ensure that the mousse is properly chilled to achieve a light and airy texture.

Enjoy your luxurious and nutty Hazelnut Praline Mousse!

White Chocolate and Lavender Panna Cotta

Ingredients:

For the Panna Cotta:

- 1 1/2 cups (360ml) heavy cream
- 1 cup (240ml) whole milk
- 1/2 cup (100g) granulated sugar
- 4 oz (115g) white chocolate, chopped
- 1 tablespoon dried culinary lavender
- 2 teaspoons gelatin powder
- 3 tablespoons water (for blooming the gelatin)

For the Lavender Syrup (optional, for drizzling):

- 1/2 cup (100g) granulated sugar
- 1/2 cup (120ml) water
- 1 tablespoon dried culinary lavender

For Garnish (optional):

- Fresh lavender sprigs
- Edible flowers
- Fresh berries

Instructions:

1. **Prepare the Lavender Infusion:**
    - In a small saucepan, heat the heavy cream and milk over medium heat until it just begins to simmer.
    - Remove from heat and add the dried lavender. Cover and steep for about 10 minutes.
    - Strain out the lavender using a fine-mesh sieve and return the cream mixture to the saucepan.
2. **Bloom the Gelatin:**
    - In a small bowl, sprinkle the gelatin powder over the water and let it sit for 5 minutes to bloom (absorb the water and swell).
3. **Make the Panna Cotta:**
    - Add the granulated sugar and chopped white chocolate to the warm cream mixture. Stir until the chocolate and sugar are fully melted and incorporated.
    - Gently heat the mixture over low heat if necessary to ensure the chocolate is completely melted.
    - Stir in the bloomed gelatin until it is fully dissolved and the mixture is smooth.
    - Remove from heat and allow the mixture to cool slightly.
4. **Pour and Chill:**
    - Pour the panna cotta mixture into individual serving glasses or molds.
    - Refrigerate for at least 4 hours, or until set. For best results, chill overnight.

5. **Prepare the Lavender Syrup (Optional):**
    - In a small saucepan, combine the granulated sugar, water, and dried lavender.
    - Bring to a simmer over medium heat, stirring until the sugar is dissolved.
    - Remove from heat and let it steep for 10 minutes, then strain out the lavender.
    - Allow the syrup to cool before using.
6. **Serve:**
    - Once the panna cotta is set, garnish with fresh lavender sprigs, edible flowers, or fresh berries if desired.
    - Drizzle with lavender syrup before serving, if using.

Tips:

- **Gelatin:** Ensure the gelatin is fully dissolved to avoid any lumps in the panna cotta.
- **Lavender:** Use culinary-grade lavender for food applications. Adjust the amount of lavender to suit your taste.
- **Serving:** If using molds, lightly oil them to help release the panna cotta easily once set.

Enjoy your elegant and fragrant White Chocolate and Lavender Panna Cotta!

Almond and Cherry Clafoutis

Ingredients:

For the Batter:

- 1 cup (240ml) whole milk
- 1/2 cup (100g) granulated sugar
- 1/2 cup (60g) all-purpose flour
- 1/4 cup (60g) almond meal (finely ground almonds)
- 3 large eggs
- 1 teaspoon vanilla extract
- 1/4 teaspoon almond extract (optional)
- 1/4 teaspoon salt
- 2 tablespoons unsalted butter, melted

For the Filling:

- 2 cups (250g) fresh or frozen cherries, pitted and halved
- 1/4 cup (30g) sliced almonds (for garnish, optional)
- Powdered sugar, for dusting (optional)

Instructions:

1. **Preheat the Oven:**
   - Preheat your oven to 375°F (190°C).
   - Grease a 9-inch (23 cm) round baking dish or a similarly sized ovenproof dish with butter.
2. **Prepare the Batter:**
   - In a large mixing bowl, whisk together the milk, granulated sugar, flour, almond meal, eggs, vanilla extract, almond extract (if using), and salt until smooth and well combined.
   - Stir in the melted butter.
3. **Prepare the Cherries:**
   - If using frozen cherries, thaw and drain them thoroughly to remove excess moisture.
   - Scatter the cherries evenly over the bottom of the prepared baking dish.
4. **Assemble and Bake:**
   - Pour the batter evenly over the cherries in the baking dish.
   - Sprinkle the sliced almonds on top of the batter if using.
   - Bake in the preheated oven for 35-45 minutes, or until the clafoutis is set and golden brown on top. A toothpick inserted into the center should come out clean.
5. **Cool and Serve:**

- Allow the clafoutis to cool slightly before serving. It can be enjoyed warm, at room temperature, or cold.
- Dust with powdered sugar just before serving, if desired.

Tips:

- **Cherry Prep:** If you prefer, you can use other fruits like berries or apples, but traditionally, clafoutis is made with cherries.
- **Texture:** The clafoutis should be somewhat custardy in the center and firm around the edges.
- **Serving:** Clafoutis is delicious on its own but can also be served with a dollop of crème fraîche or vanilla ice cream.

Enjoy your charming and flavorful Almond and Cherry Clafoutis!

Dark Chocolate and Sea Salt Tart

Ingredients:

For the Tart Crust:

- 1 1/4 cups (160g) all-purpose flour
- 1/4 cup (50g) granulated sugar
- 1/2 teaspoon salt
- 1/2 cup (115g) unsalted butter, cold and cut into small cubes
- 1 large egg yolk
- 2 tablespoons ice water (as needed)

For the Dark Chocolate Filling:

- 1 cup (240ml) heavy cream
- 8 oz (225g) dark chocolate (70% cocoa), chopped
- 2 tablespoons unsalted butter
- 1 teaspoon vanilla extract
- 1/4 teaspoon sea salt, plus more for garnish

Instructions:

1. **Prepare the Tart Crust:**
   - Preheat your oven to 350°F (175°C).
   - In a food processor, combine the flour, granulated sugar, and salt. Pulse to combine.
   - Add the cold butter and pulse until the mixture resembles coarse crumbs.
   - Add the egg yolk and pulse until the dough begins to come together. If needed, add ice water, a little at a time, until the dough holds together when pressed.
   - Turn the dough out onto a lightly floured surface and gently knead it a few times to bring it together. Flatten into a disk, wrap in plastic wrap, and chill in the refrigerator for at least 30 minutes.
2. **Bake the Tart Crust:**
   - Roll out the chilled dough on a floured surface to fit a 9-inch (23 cm) tart pan with a removable bottom. Transfer the dough to the tart pan, pressing it into the edges and trimming any excess.
   - Chill the dough in the pan for another 15 minutes.
   - Line the tart shell with parchment paper and fill with pie weights or dried beans.
   - Bake for 15 minutes. Remove the parchment paper and weights, and bake for an additional 10 minutes, or until the crust is golden brown. Let cool completely.
3. **Prepare the Dark Chocolate Filling:**
   - In a medium saucepan, heat the heavy cream over medium heat until it just begins to simmer. Remove from heat.

    - Add the chopped dark chocolate and let it sit for 1-2 minutes to soften.
    - Stir the mixture until smooth and fully combined.
    - Add the butter and vanilla extract, stirring until the butter is melted and the filling is glossy.
    - Stir in the 1/4 teaspoon of sea salt.
4. **Assemble the Tart:**
    - Pour the dark chocolate filling into the cooled tart shell, spreading it evenly with a spatula.
    - Refrigerate for at least 2 hours, or until the filling is set.
5. **Garnish and Serve:**
    - Before serving, sprinkle the tart with a little extra sea salt for garnish.
    - Slice and serve chilled. The tart can be stored in the refrigerator for up to 1 week.

Tips:

- **Crust:** Ensure the tart crust is well-chilled before baking to avoid shrinking. The blind-baking process helps to keep it crisp.
- **Chocolate:** Use high-quality dark chocolate for the best flavor and smooth texture.
- **Sea Salt:** Use flaky sea salt for a more refined taste and attractive presentation.

Enjoy your rich and indulgent Dark Chocolate and Sea Salt Tart!

Passion Fruit and Mango Panna Cotta

Ingredients:

For the Panna Cotta:

- 1 cup (240ml) heavy cream
- 1 cup (240ml) whole milk
- 1/2 cup (100g) granulated sugar
- 2 teaspoons gelatin powder
- 3 tablespoons water (for blooming the gelatin)
- 1 teaspoon vanilla extract

For the Passion Fruit and Mango Sauce:

- 1/2 cup (120ml) passion fruit juice (fresh or store-bought)
- 1/2 cup (120ml) mango puree (fresh or store-bought)
- 2 tablespoons granulated sugar
- 1 tablespoon cornstarch mixed with 2 tablespoons water (optional, for thickening)

For Garnish (optional):

- Fresh mint leaves
- Mango cubes
- Passion fruit seeds

Instructions:

1. **Prepare the Panna Cotta:**
    - In a small bowl, sprinkle the gelatin over the water and let it sit for about 5 minutes to bloom.
    - In a medium saucepan, combine the heavy cream, whole milk, and granulated sugar. Heat over medium heat until the sugar is dissolved and the mixture is hot but not boiling.
    - Remove from heat and stir in the bloomed gelatin until fully dissolved. Add the vanilla extract and mix well.
    - Pour the mixture into individual serving glasses or molds.
    - Refrigerate for at least 4 hours, or until fully set. For best results, chill overnight.
2. **Prepare the Passion Fruit and Mango Sauce:**
    - In a small saucepan, combine the passion fruit juice, mango puree, and granulated sugar.
    - Heat over medium heat until the sugar is dissolved and the mixture is warmed through.
    - If you prefer a thicker sauce, stir in the cornstarch mixture and cook for an additional 2-3 minutes, or until the sauce thickens slightly.

- Remove from heat and let the sauce cool to room temperature.
3. **Assemble and Serve:**
    - Once the panna cotta is set, gently spoon or drizzle the passion fruit and mango sauce over the top.
    - Garnish with fresh mint leaves, mango cubes, and passion fruit seeds if desired.

Tips:

- **Gelatin:** Make sure the gelatin is fully dissolved to avoid lumps in the panna cotta.
- **Fruit Puree:** If using fresh mango, blend ripe mango flesh to make the puree. You can also use store-bought puree if fresh mango is not available.
- **Serving:** For a more elegant presentation, you can unmold the panna cotta onto serving plates. Lightly oil the molds before pouring in the panna cotta to make unmolding easier.

Enjoy your refreshing and tropical Passion Fruit and Mango Panna Cotta!

Bourbon Pecan Pie with Bourbon Caramel Sauce

Ingredients:

For the Pie Crust:

- 1 1/4 cups (160g) all-purpose flour
- 1/4 cup (50g) granulated sugar
- 1/4 teaspoon salt
- 1/2 cup (115g) unsalted butter, cold and cut into small cubes
- 1 large egg yolk
- 2-3 tablespoons ice water

For the Pecan Pie Filling:

- 1 cup (240ml) light corn syrup
- 1 cup (220g) packed brown sugar
- 1/2 cup (115g) unsalted butter, melted
- 1/4 cup (60ml) bourbon
- 4 large eggs
- 1 1/2 cups (180g) pecan halves
- 1 teaspoon vanilla extract
- 1/4 teaspoon salt

For the Bourbon Caramel Sauce:

- 1 cup (200g) granulated sugar
- 6 tablespoons unsalted butter, cut into pieces
- 1/2 cup (120ml) heavy cream
- 1/4 cup (60ml) bourbon
- Pinch of salt

Instructions:

1. **Prepare the Pie Crust:**
    - In a food processor, combine the flour, granulated sugar, and salt. Pulse to mix.
    - Add the cold butter and pulse until the mixture resembles coarse crumbs.
    - Add the egg yolk and pulse until the dough starts to come together. If necessary, add ice water, one tablespoon at a time, until the dough holds together when pressed.
    - Turn the dough out onto a lightly floured surface and gently knead it a few times. Flatten into a disk, wrap in plastic wrap, and refrigerate for at least 30 minutes.
2. **Bake the Pie Crust:**
    - Preheat your oven to 375°F (190°C).

- Roll out the chilled dough on a floured surface to fit a 9-inch (23 cm) pie pan. Transfer the dough to the pan, pressing it into the edges and trimming any excess.
- Line the crust with parchment paper and fill with pie weights or dried beans.
- Bake for 15 minutes. Remove the parchment paper and weights, and bake for an additional 10 minutes, or until the crust is lightly golden. Let cool slightly.

3. **Prepare the Pecan Pie Filling:**
   - In a large bowl, whisk together the corn syrup, brown sugar, melted butter, bourbon, eggs, vanilla extract, and salt until well combined.
   - Stir in the pecan halves.
   - Pour the filling into the pre-baked pie crust.

4. **Bake the Pecan Pie:**
   - Bake at 375°F (190°C) for 45-55 minutes, or until the filling is set and the top is golden brown. The center should still be slightly jiggly.
   - Allow the pie to cool completely on a wire rack before serving.

5. **Prepare the Bourbon Caramel Sauce:**
   - In a medium saucepan, heat the granulated sugar over medium heat, stirring constantly until it melts and turns an amber color.
   - Carefully add the butter (the mixture will bubble up) and stir until fully melted and combined.
   - Gradually add the heavy cream, stirring constantly. The mixture will bubble again.
   - Stir in the bourbon and a pinch of salt. Remove from heat and let cool slightly before serving.

6. **Serve:**
   - Slice the cooled pecan pie and drizzle with bourbon caramel sauce just before serving.

Tips:

- **Pie Crust:** To avoid a soggy crust, ensure it's fully pre-baked and cooled before adding the filling.
- **Caramel Sauce:** The bourbon can be adjusted based on taste. If you prefer a stronger bourbon flavor, add more bourbon after the sauce has been removed from heat.
- **Cooling Time:** Let the pie cool completely to allow the filling to set properly.

Enjoy your rich and flavorful Bourbon Pecan Pie with Bourbon Caramel Sauce!

Coconut and Lime Rice Pudding

Ingredients:

- 1 cup (200g) Arborio rice or short-grain rice
- 1 can (13.5 oz or 400ml) coconut milk
- 2 cups (480ml) whole milk
- 1/2 cup (100g) granulated sugar
- 1/4 teaspoon salt
- 1 tablespoon lime zest (from about 2 limes)
- 1/4 cup (60ml) freshly squeezed lime juice (from about 2 limes)
- 1 teaspoon vanilla extract
- 1/4 cup (50g) shredded sweetened coconut (optional, for garnish)
- Fresh mint leaves (optional, for garnish)

Instructions:

1. **Cook the Rice:**
   - In a medium saucepan, combine the rice, coconut milk, whole milk, granulated sugar, and salt.
   - Bring the mixture to a boil over medium-high heat, stirring occasionally.
   - Reduce the heat to low and simmer, stirring frequently, for about 20-25 minutes, or until the rice is tender and the mixture has thickened to a creamy consistency.
2. **Add Flavors:**
   - Stir in the lime zest and lime juice. Cook for an additional 2-3 minutes, allowing the flavors to meld.
   - Remove the saucepan from heat and stir in the vanilla extract.
3. **Cool and Serve:**
   - Transfer the rice pudding to serving bowls or glasses.
   - Allow it to cool to room temperature, then refrigerate for at least 2 hours to chill and set.
   - Just before serving, garnish with shredded coconut and fresh mint leaves, if desired.

Tips:

- **Rice:** Arborio rice or any short-grain rice works well for a creamy texture. If using long-grain rice, you may need to adjust the cooking time and liquid.
- **Sweetness:** Adjust the sugar to taste, depending on how sweet you like your rice pudding.
- **Garnish:** Toasting the shredded coconut before using can add extra flavor and texture.

Enjoy your Coconut and Lime Rice Pudding as a delightful and tropical treat!

Fig and Walnut Tart with Honey Glaze

Ingredients:

For the Tart Crust:

- 1 1/4 cups (160g) all-purpose flour
- 1/4 cup (50g) granulated sugar
- 1/4 teaspoon salt
- 1/2 cup (115g) unsalted butter, cold and cut into small cubes
- 1 large egg yolk
- 2-3 tablespoons ice water

For the Filling:

- 1 cup (100g) walnuts, roughly chopped
- 1 cup (200g) dried figs, chopped
- 1/2 cup (100g) brown sugar
- 1/4 cup (60ml) honey
- 1/4 cup (60ml) heavy cream
- 2 large eggs
- 1 teaspoon vanilla extract
- 1/4 teaspoon salt

For the Honey Glaze:

- 1/4 cup (60ml) honey
- 2 tablespoons water

Instructions:

1. **Prepare the Tart Crust:**
    - In a food processor, combine the flour, granulated sugar, and salt. Pulse to mix.
    - Add the cold butter and pulse until the mixture resembles coarse crumbs.
    - Add the egg yolk and pulse until the dough starts to come together. If necessary, add ice water, one tablespoon at a time, until the dough holds together when pressed.
    - Turn the dough out onto a lightly floured surface and gently knead it a few times. Flatten into a disk, wrap in plastic wrap, and refrigerate for at least 30 minutes.
2. **Bake the Tart Crust:**
    - Preheat your oven to 375°F (190°C).
    - Roll out the chilled dough on a floured surface to fit a 9-inch (23 cm) tart pan with a removable bottom. Transfer the dough to the pan, pressing it into the edges and trimming any excess.
    - Line the crust with parchment paper and fill with pie weights or dried beans.

- Bake for 15 minutes. Remove the parchment paper and weights, and bake for an additional 10 minutes, or until the crust is golden brown. Let cool slightly.
3. **Prepare the Filling:**
    - In a medium bowl, combine the chopped walnuts and figs.
    - In a separate bowl, whisk together the brown sugar, honey, heavy cream, eggs, vanilla extract, and salt until smooth.
    - Pour the sugar mixture over the walnut and fig mixture, stirring to combine.
    - Pour the filling into the pre-baked tart shell.
4. **Bake the Tart:**
    - Bake at 375°F (190°C) for 25-30 minutes, or until the filling is set and the top is golden brown.
    - Allow the tart to cool completely on a wire rack.
5. **Prepare the Honey Glaze:**
    - In a small saucepan, combine the honey and water.
    - Heat over low heat, stirring until the honey is thinned and the mixture is smooth.
    - Remove from heat and let cool slightly.
6. **Glaze and Serve:**
    - Brush the honey glaze over the cooled tart.
    - Garnish with additional chopped walnuts if desired.
    - Slice and serve at room temperature.

Tips:

- **Tart Crust:** Ensure the tart crust is well-chilled before baking to prevent shrinking.
- **Filling:** The tart will continue to set as it cools, so allow it to cool completely before slicing.
- **Honey Glaze:** For a more intense honey flavor, you can reduce the glaze slightly before brushing it onto the tart.

Enjoy your elegant and delicious Fig and Walnut Tart with Honey Glaze!

Mascarpone and Berry Parfait

Ingredients:

For the Mascarpone Layer:

- 1 cup (250g) mascarpone cheese
- 1/2 cup (120ml) heavy cream
- 1/4 cup (50g) granulated sugar
- 1 teaspoon vanilla extract

For the Berry Layer:

- 1 cup (150g) mixed fresh berries (such as strawberries, blueberries, raspberries, and blackberries)
- 2 tablespoons granulated sugar
- 1 tablespoon lemon juice (optional, for added brightness)

For the Garnish (optional):

- Fresh mint leaves
- Granola or crushed nuts
- Additional berries

Instructions:

1. **Prepare the Berry Layer:**
    - In a medium bowl, combine the fresh berries, granulated sugar, and lemon juice (if using).
    - Gently toss to coat the berries with the sugar and lemon juice. Let them sit for about 10-15 minutes to macerate, which will release their natural juices.
2. **Prepare the Mascarpone Layer:**
    - In a medium bowl, whisk together the mascarpone cheese, heavy cream, granulated sugar, and vanilla extract until smooth and creamy. You can use an electric mixer if you prefer a lighter, more aerated texture.
3. **Assemble the Parfaits:**
    - In serving glasses or bowls, spoon a layer of the mascarpone mixture.
    - Top with a layer of the macerated berries.
    - Repeat the layers until the glasses are filled, ending with a layer of berries on top.
4. **Garnish and Serve:**
    - Garnish with fresh mint leaves, granola, or crushed nuts if desired.
    - Serve immediately or chill in the refrigerator for up to 2 hours before serving.

Tips:

- **Mascarpone Mixture:** For a lighter texture, you can fold in some whipped cream into the mascarpone mixture.
- **Berry Variations:** Feel free to use your favorite berries or even a berry compote for the fruit layer.
- **Make Ahead:** You can prepare the parfaits a few hours in advance and keep them refrigerated. However, it's best to add crunchy garnishes like granola just before serving to keep them crisp.

Enjoy your Mascarpone and Berry Parfait, a fresh and creamy dessert with a burst of berry flavor!

Pomegranate and Mint Granita

Ingredients:

- 2 cups (480ml) pomegranate juice (freshly squeezed or store-bought)
- 1/2 cup (100g) granulated sugar
- 1/4 cup (60ml) water
- 1/4 cup (60ml) freshly squeezed lemon juice (about 1 lemon)
- 1/4 cup (60ml) finely chopped fresh mint leaves
- Mint sprigs, for garnish (optional)

Instructions:

1. **Prepare the Simple Syrup:**
   - In a small saucepan, combine the granulated sugar and water.
   - Heat over medium heat, stirring until the sugar is completely dissolved. Remove from heat and let it cool to room temperature.
2. **Combine Ingredients:**
   - In a large bowl, mix the pomegranate juice, cooled simple syrup, and lemon juice.
   - Stir in the finely chopped mint leaves.
3. **Freeze the Granita:**
   - Pour the mixture into a shallow baking dish.
   - Place the dish in the freezer. After about 30 minutes, use a fork to scrape and stir the mixture to break up any ice crystals. Return to the freezer.
   - Continue to scrape and stir every 30 minutes for about 2-3 hours, or until the granita is fully frozen and has a fluffy, granular texture.
4. **Serve:**
   - Before serving, use a fork to fluff the granita once more.
   - Spoon the granita into serving glasses or bowls.
   - Garnish with mint sprigs if desired.

Tips:

- **Mint Flavor:** If you prefer a stronger mint flavor, you can steep the chopped mint leaves in the simple syrup for a few minutes before cooling and adding to the mixture.
- **Texture:** The key to a perfect granita is the frequent scraping and stirring, which helps achieve a light, fluffy texture.
- **Serving:** Granita is best served immediately after scraping. If it sits too long, it may become too hard; just re-scrape to restore the texture.

Enjoy your Pomegranate and Mint Granita—a beautifully refreshing and aromatic frozen treat!

Raspberry Macarons with Lemon Filling

Ingredients:

For the Raspberry Macarons:

- 1 1/2 cups (150g) powdered sugar
- 1 cup (100g) almond flour
- 1/4 cup (50g) granulated sugar
- 3 large egg whites, at room temperature
- 1/4 teaspoon cream of tartar
- 1/2 teaspoon vanilla extract
- Red or pink food coloring (optional)
- 1/2 cup (70g) freeze-dried raspberries, finely ground (for flavor and color)

For the Lemon Filling:

- 1/2 cup (115g) unsalted butter, softened
- 1 cup (120g) powdered sugar
- 2 tablespoons lemon juice (freshly squeezed)
- 1 teaspoon lemon zest
- 1/2 teaspoon vanilla extract

Instructions:

1. **Prepare the Macaron Shells:**
    - **Preheat Oven:** Preheat your oven to 300°F (150°C). Line two baking sheets with parchment paper or silicone baking mats.
    - **Sift Dry Ingredients:** In a medium bowl, sift together the powdered sugar, almond flour, and ground freeze-dried raspberries. Set aside.
    - **Whip Egg Whites:** In a clean, dry mixing bowl, use an electric mixer to beat the egg whites with the cream of tartar until soft peaks form.
    - **Add Sugar:** Gradually add the granulated sugar, beating continuously until stiff, glossy peaks form.
    - **Add Flavor and Color:** Gently fold in the vanilla extract and a few drops of food coloring (if using).
    - **Incorporate Dry Ingredients:** Fold the sifted dry ingredients into the meringue mixture in three additions. Use a spatula to gently fold until the batter flows smoothly and forms a ribbon when drizzled from the spatula.
    - **Pipe the Shells:** Transfer the batter to a piping bag fitted with a round tip. Pipe small circles (about 1 to 1.5 inches in diameter) onto the prepared baking sheets, spacing them about 1 inch apart.
    - **Rest the Shells:** Tap the baking sheets on the counter to release air bubbles and allow the piped macaron batter to rest for about 30 minutes, or until a skin forms on the surface.

- **Bake:** Bake in the preheated oven for 15-18 minutes, or until the macarons have risen and have a firm base. Let them cool completely on the baking sheets before removing.

2. **Prepare the Lemon Filling:**
   - **Beat Butter:** In a mixing bowl, beat the softened butter with an electric mixer until creamy and smooth.
   - **Add Sugar:** Gradually add the powdered sugar, beating until combined.
   - **Add Lemon:** Mix in the lemon juice, lemon zest, and vanilla extract. Continue to beat until the filling is light and fluffy.
3. **Assemble the Macarons:**
   - **Pair Shells:** Match the macaron shells into pairs of similar size.
   - **Fill:** Transfer the lemon filling to a piping bag fitted with a round tip. Pipe a small amount of filling onto the flat side of one shell of each pair.
   - **Sandwich:** Gently press the other shell on top to form a sandwich.
4. **Chill and Serve:**
   - **Chill:** Place the assembled macarons in an airtight container and refrigerate for at least 24 hours to allow the flavors to meld and the filling to set.
   - **Serve:** Allow the macarons to come to room temperature before serving.

Tips:

- **Meringue:** Ensure your mixing bowl and beaters are completely clean and free of grease for the best meringue.
- **Macaronage:** Be careful not to over-mix the batter. The macaronage process should be done gently to achieve the right consistency.
- **Freeze-dried Raspberries:** Use finely ground freeze-dried raspberries for best results. They add both flavor and color without adding moisture to the batter.

Enjoy your Raspberry Macarons with Lemon Filling—these delicate treats are sure to impress!

Spiced Apple Compote with Cinnamon Gelato

Ingredients:

For the Spiced Apple Compote:

- 4 medium apples (such as Granny Smith or Honeycrisp), peeled, cored, and diced
- 1/4 cup (50g) granulated sugar
- 1/4 cup (60ml) apple cider
- 1/2 teaspoon ground cinnamon
- 1/4 teaspoon ground nutmeg
- 1/4 teaspoon ground allspice
- 1 tablespoon lemon juice
- 1 tablespoon unsalted butter

For the Cinnamon Gelato:

- 2 cups (480ml) whole milk
- 1 cup (240ml) heavy cream
- 3/4 cup (150g) granulated sugar
- 1/2 cup (120ml) whole milk powder
- 4 large egg yolks
- 1 tablespoon ground cinnamon
- 1 teaspoon vanilla extract

Instructions:

1. **Prepare the Spiced Apple Compote:**
   - **Cook Apples:** In a medium saucepan, melt the butter over medium heat. Add the diced apples and cook, stirring occasionally, for about 5 minutes, or until they start to soften.
   - **Add Spices and Liquid:** Stir in the granulated sugar, apple cider, ground cinnamon, nutmeg, and allspice. Cook for an additional 10 minutes, or until the apples are tender and the mixture has thickened slightly.
   - **Finish:** Stir in the lemon juice and cook for another 2 minutes. Remove from heat and let the compote cool to room temperature. It can be served warm or chilled.
2. **Prepare the Cinnamon Gelato:**
   - **Heat Dairy:** In a medium saucepan, heat the whole milk and heavy cream over medium heat until it begins to steam. Do not let it boil.
   - **Mix Dry Ingredients:** In a separate bowl, whisk together the granulated sugar, milk powder, and ground cinnamon.
   - **Prepare Egg Yolks:** In another bowl, whisk the egg yolks until they are light and slightly thickened.

- **Temper Eggs:** Gradually add a small amount of the hot milk mixture to the egg yolks, whisking constantly to temper them. Once combined, slowly whisk the egg yolk mixture back into the saucepan with the remaining milk mixture.
- **Cook Custard:** Cook over medium heat, stirring constantly, until the mixture thickens and coats the back of a spoon (170-175°F or 77-80°C).
- **Cool and Chill:** Remove from heat and stir in the vanilla extract. Strain the mixture through a fine-mesh sieve into a clean bowl. Let it cool to room temperature, then cover and refrigerate for at least 4 hours, or overnight.

3. **Churn the Gelato:**
    - **Churn:** Once the custard base is chilled, pour it into an ice cream maker and churn according to the manufacturer's instructions until it reaches a soft-serve consistency.
    - **Freeze:** Transfer the gelato to a container and freeze for at least 2 hours to firm up.
4. **Serve:**
    - **Dish Up:** Spoon the spiced apple compote into serving bowls.
    - **Top with Gelato:** Add a scoop of cinnamon gelato on top of each serving of apple compote.
    - **Garnish:** Optionally, garnish with a sprinkle of additional cinnamon or a few extra apple slices.

Tips:

- **Apples:** Choose firm apples that hold their shape well when cooked.
- **Gelato Consistency:** If you don't have an ice cream maker, you can place the mixture in a shallow dish and stir every 30 minutes until it reaches a gelato-like consistency.
- **Spices:** Adjust the spices in the apple compote according to your taste preferences.

Enjoy your Spiced Apple Compote with Cinnamon Gelato—a perfect combination of warm and cool flavors that's sure to delight!

Chocolate Lava Cake with Raspberry Coulis

Ingredients:

For the Chocolate Lava Cake:

- 1/2 cup (115g) unsalted butter, plus extra for greasing
- 4 ounces (115g) bittersweet or semisweet chocolate, chopped
- 1 cup (120g) powdered sugar
- 2 large eggs
- 2 large egg yolks
- 1 teaspoon vanilla extract
- 1/2 cup (65g) all-purpose flour
- Pinch of salt

For the Raspberry Coulis:

- 1 cup (150g) fresh or frozen raspberries
- 1/2 cup (100g) granulated sugar
- 1/4 cup (60ml) water
- 1 teaspoon lemon juice (optional, for brightness)

For Garnish (optional):

- Fresh raspberries
- Mint leaves
- Powdered sugar

Instructions:

1. **Prepare the Raspberry Coulis:**
   - **Cook Raspberries:** In a medium saucepan, combine the raspberries, granulated sugar, and water.
   - **Simmer:** Cook over medium heat, stirring occasionally, until the raspberries break down and the mixture thickens (about 10 minutes).
   - **Blend:** Remove from heat and let it cool slightly. Blend the mixture with an immersion blender or in a regular blender until smooth.
   - **Strain:** Strain the sauce through a fine-mesh sieve to remove the seeds, if desired. Stir in lemon juice, if using. Allow the coulis to cool completely.
2. **Prepare the Chocolate Lava Cakes:**
   - **Preheat Oven:** Preheat your oven to 425°F (220°C). Grease 4 ramekins with butter and lightly dust with flour or cocoa powder.
   - **Melt Chocolate:** In a microwave-safe bowl or using a double boiler, melt the butter and chopped chocolate together until smooth. Stir until well combined.

- **Mix Sugar and Eggs:** In a medium bowl, whisk together the powdered sugar, eggs, egg yolks, and vanilla extract until smooth and well combined.
- **Combine:** Fold the melted chocolate mixture into the egg mixture until fully incorporated.
- **Add Flour:** Gently fold in the flour and a pinch of salt until just combined. Be careful not to overmix.
- **Pour Batter:** Divide the batter evenly among the prepared ramekins.
- **Bake:** Bake in the preheated oven for 12-14 minutes, or until the edges are set but the centers are still soft and slightly jiggly.
- **Cool:** Allow the cakes to cool in the ramekins for 1-2 minutes, then run a knife around the edges to loosen. Invert the cakes onto serving plates.

3. **Serve:**
    - **Plate:** Spoon some raspberry coulis onto each plate.
    - **Top:** Place a chocolate lava cake on top of the coulis.
    - **Garnish:** Optionally, garnish with fresh raspberries, mint leaves, and a dusting of powdered sugar.

Tips:

- **Ramekins:** Make sure your ramekins are well-greased to prevent sticking.
- **Timing:** Be careful not to over-bake the cakes; the centers should remain molten for the classic lava effect.
- **Serving:** Serve immediately after baking for the best lava effect, as the centers will set as they cool.

Enjoy your indulgent Chocolate Lava Cake with Raspberry Coulis—an elegant and delicious dessert that's sure to impress!

Caramelized Pear and Almond Tart

Ingredients:

For the Tart Crust:

- 1 1/4 cups (160g) all-purpose flour
- 1/4 cup (50g) granulated sugar
- 1/4 teaspoon salt
- 1/2 cup (115g) unsalted butter, cold and cut into small cubes
- 1 large egg yolk
- 2-3 tablespoons ice water

For the Almond Filling (Frangipane):

- 1/2 cup (115g) unsalted butter, softened
- 1/2 cup (100g) granulated sugar
- 1 cup (100g) almond meal or ground almonds
- 2 large eggs
- 1 teaspoon vanilla extract
- 1 tablespoon all-purpose flour

For the Caramelized Pears:

- 4 ripe pears, peeled, cored, and sliced thinly
- 1/4 cup (50g) granulated sugar
- 2 tablespoons unsalted butter
- 1 tablespoon lemon juice

For the Glaze (optional):

- 1/4 cup (60ml) apricot jam
- 1 tablespoon water

Instructions:

1. **Prepare the Tart Crust:**
    - **Mix Dry Ingredients:** In a medium bowl, whisk together the flour, granulated sugar, and salt.
    - **Cut in Butter:** Add the cold butter and use a pastry cutter or your fingers to cut it into the flour mixture until it resembles coarse crumbs.
    - **Add Egg Yolk:** Mix in the egg yolk and 2 tablespoons of ice water. Stir until the dough starts to come together. If the dough is too dry, add an additional tablespoon of ice water.

- **Chill Dough:** Turn the dough out onto a lightly floured surface and knead it a few times to bring it together. Flatten into a disk, wrap in plastic wrap, and refrigerate for at least 30 minutes.

2. **Prepare the Almond Filling:**
   - **Cream Butter and Sugar:** In a medium bowl, beat together the softened butter and granulated sugar until light and creamy.
   - **Add Almonds and Eggs:** Mix in the almond meal, then add the eggs one at a time, beating well after each addition. Stir in the vanilla extract and flour until fully combined.

3. **Prepare the Caramelized Pears:**
   - **Cook Pears:** In a large skillet, melt the butter over medium heat. Add the granulated sugar and cook until it starts to caramelize and turn golden brown.
   - **Add Pears:** Add the pear slices and lemon juice to the skillet. Cook, stirring occasionally, until the pears are tender and caramelized, about 10 minutes. Remove from heat and let cool slightly.

4. **Assemble the Tart:**
   - **Preheat Oven:** Preheat your oven to 375°F (190°C).
   - **Roll Out Dough:** On a lightly floured surface, roll out the chilled dough to fit a 9-inch (23 cm) tart pan with a removable bottom. Transfer the dough to the pan, pressing it into the edges and trimming any excess.
   - **Pre-Bake Crust:** Line the crust with parchment paper and fill with pie weights or dried beans. Bake for 15 minutes, then remove the parchment paper and weights and bake for an additional 5 minutes, or until lightly golden. Let cool slightly.
   - **Add Almond Filling:** Spread the almond filling evenly over the pre-baked tart crust.
   - **Arrange Pears:** Arrange the caramelized pear slices on top of the almond filling in a decorative pattern.

5. **Bake the Tart:**
   - **Bake:** Bake the tart in the preheated oven for 25-30 minutes, or until the almond filling is set and golden brown.
   - **Cool:** Allow the tart to cool in the pan for 10 minutes before transferring to a wire rack to cool completely.

6. **Glaze (Optional):**
   - **Prepare Glaze:** In a small saucepan, heat the apricot jam and water until melted and smooth. Strain if necessary.
   - **Glaze Tart:** Brush the glaze over the cooled tart for a shiny finish.

Tips:

- **Dough:** Ensure the tart dough is well-chilled before rolling out to prevent shrinkage during baking.
- **Pears:** For the best caramelization, make sure the pears are not too ripe.
- **Frangipane:** The almond filling can be prepared a day in advance and kept in the refrigerator.

Enjoy your Caramelized Pear and Almond Tart—a deliciously elegant dessert that's sure to impress!

Vanilla Bean Crème Brûlée with Fresh Berries

Ingredients:

For the Crème Brûlée:

- 2 cups (480ml) heavy cream
- 1 vanilla bean (or 1 tablespoon vanilla extract if you don't have a vanilla bean)
- 5 large egg yolks
- 1/2 cup (100g) granulated sugar
- 1/4 cup (50g) brown sugar (for topping)

For the Fresh Berries:

- 1 cup (150g) mixed fresh berries (such as raspberries, strawberries, blueberries, and blackberries)

Instructions:

1. **Prepare the Vanilla Bean Crème Brûlée:**
    - **Preheat Oven:** Preheat your oven to 325°F (160°C).
    - **Heat Cream:** In a medium saucepan, heat the heavy cream over medium heat until it begins to steam. If using a vanilla bean, split the bean lengthwise with a knife and scrape the seeds into the cream. Add the vanilla bean pod as well. If using vanilla extract, add it later. Remove from heat and let it steep for 10 minutes. Remove and discard the vanilla bean pod if used.
    - **Whisk Egg Yolks and Sugar:** In a medium bowl, whisk together the egg yolks and granulated sugar until pale and slightly thickened.
    - **Combine:** Gradually pour the warm cream into the egg yolk mixture, whisking continuously to prevent curdling. If using vanilla extract, stir it in now.
    - **Strain Custard:** Strain the mixture through a fine-mesh sieve into a clean bowl or large measuring cup to ensure a smooth custard.
2. **Bake the Crème Brûlée:**
    - **Prepare Ramekins:** Place 4-6 ramekins (depending on size) in a baking dish. Pour the custard mixture evenly into the ramekins.
    - **Create a Water Bath:** Carefully pour hot water into the baking dish around the ramekins, making sure it comes about halfway up the sides of the ramekins.
    - **Bake:** Bake in the preheated oven for 30-40 minutes, or until the custards are set around the edges but still slightly jiggly in the center.
    - **Cool:** Remove the ramekins from the water bath and let them cool to room temperature. Refrigerate for at least 2 hours, or until well chilled.
3. **Caramelize the Sugar:**
    - **Prepare Topping:** Just before serving, sprinkle a thin, even layer of brown sugar over the top of each custard.

- **Caramelize:** Using a kitchen torch, carefully caramelize the sugar until it forms a crisp, golden-brown crust. If you don't have a torch, you can place the ramekins under a broiler set to high for 1-2 minutes, but watch closely to prevent burning.
4. **Serve:**
    - **Garnish:** Serve the crème brûlée immediately after caramelizing. Garnish with fresh berries on the side or on top.

Tips:

- **Vanilla Bean:** Using a vanilla bean provides a more intense and authentic vanilla flavor, but vanilla extract works well if you're short on time.
- **Torch Use:** A kitchen torch is ideal for caramelizing the sugar as it allows precise control. If using the broiler, be very careful as the sugar can burn quickly.
- **Texture:** The custard should be creamy and smooth, with a crisp caramelized sugar topping. If the custard is overcooked, it may be grainy.

Enjoy your Vanilla Bean Crème Brûlée with Fresh Berries—a perfect combination of creamy, crispy, and fruity flavors for a truly indulgent dessert!

Mocha Tiramisu with Coffee Soaked Cake

Ingredients:

For the Coffee-Soaked Cake:

- 1 cup (240ml) strong brewed coffee, cooled
- 2 tablespoons coffee liqueur (optional)
- 1/2 cup (100g) granulated sugar
- 3 large eggs
- 1/2 cup (115g) unsalted butter, melted
- 1 cup (125g) all-purpose flour
- 1/2 teaspoon baking powder
- 1/4 teaspoon salt
- 1 tablespoon cocoa powder

For the Mocha Mascarpone Mixture:

- 8 ounces (225g) mascarpone cheese, softened
- 1 cup (240ml) heavy cream
- 1/2 cup (50g) powdered sugar
- 2 tablespoons unsweetened cocoa powder
- 2 tablespoons coffee liqueur (optional)
- 1/2 cup (120ml) strong brewed coffee, cooled
- 2 tablespoons instant coffee granules
- 1 teaspoon vanilla extract

For Garnish:

- Unsweetened cocoa powder, for dusting
- Chocolate shavings or grated chocolate

Instructions:

1. **Prepare the Coffee-Soaked Cake:**
   - **Preheat Oven:** Preheat your oven to 350°F (175°C). Grease and flour an 8-inch (20 cm) round cake pan.
   - **Mix Wet Ingredients:** In a medium bowl, whisk together the brewed coffee, coffee liqueur (if using), and granulated sugar until the sugar is dissolved.
   - **Mix Dry Ingredients:** In another bowl, whisk together the flour, baking powder, salt, and cocoa powder.
   - **Combine:** Add the eggs and melted butter to the coffee mixture, and mix until combined. Gradually add the dry ingredients, mixing until just combined.
   - **Bake:** Pour the batter into the prepared cake pan. Bake for 20-25 minutes, or until a toothpick inserted into the center comes out clean.

- **Cool:** Allow the cake to cool in the pan for 10 minutes, then transfer to a wire rack to cool completely.
2. **Prepare the Mocha Mascarpone Mixture:**
    - **Whip Cream:** In a large mixing bowl, whip the heavy cream with an electric mixer until soft peaks form.
    - **Mix Mascarpone:** In another bowl, beat the mascarpone cheese, powdered sugar, cocoa powder, coffee liqueur (if using), and instant coffee granules until smooth and creamy.
    - **Combine:** Gently fold the whipped cream into the mascarpone mixture until well combined. Stir in the vanilla extract and cooled brewed coffee.
3. **Assemble the Tiramisu:**
    - **Soak Cake:** Cut the cooled cake into slices or cubes. Dip each piece quickly into the coffee mixture (combine the brewed coffee with a bit more coffee liqueur if desired).
    - **Layer:** In a serving dish (a 9x9-inch square dish or similar), create a layer of the soaked cake. Spread a layer of the mocha mascarpone mixture over the cake. Repeat the layers, ending with the mascarpone mixture on top.
    - **Chill:** Cover and refrigerate for at least 4 hours, or overnight, to allow the flavors to meld and the dessert to set.
4. **Garnish and Serve:**
    - **Dust:** Just before serving, dust the top with unsweetened cocoa powder and garnish with chocolate shavings or grated chocolate if desired.
    - **Serve:** Cut into squares and serve chilled.

Tips:

- **Coffee Soaking:** Do not soak the cake pieces too long; they should be moist but not soggy.
- **Mascarpone Mixture:** Ensure the mascarpone is softened for a smooth, creamy texture.
- **Make Ahead:** Tiramisu tastes even better the next day as the flavors have more time to develop.

Enjoy your Mocha Tiramisu with Coffee-Soaked Cake—a deliciously rich and indulgent dessert that's perfect for coffee and chocolate lovers alike!

Orange Blossom and Honey Cheesecake

Ingredients:

For the Crust:

- 1 1/2 cups (150g) graham cracker crumbs
- 1/4 cup (50g) granulated sugar
- 1/2 cup (115g) unsalted butter, melted

For the Cheesecake Filling:

- 3 (8-ounce) packages (675g total) cream cheese, softened
- 1 cup (240ml) sour cream
- 1 cup (240ml) heavy cream
- 1 cup (240g) honey
- 1/2 cup (100g) granulated sugar
- 3 large eggs
- 2 tablespoons all-purpose flour
- 2 tablespoons orange blossom water
- 1 teaspoon vanilla extract
- Zest of 1 orange

For the Honey Glaze (optional):

- 1/4 cup (60ml) honey
- 1 tablespoon water

For Garnish (optional):

- Orange zest
- Fresh mint leaves

Instructions:

1. **Prepare the Crust:**
   - **Preheat Oven:** Preheat your oven to 350°F (175°C).
   - **Mix Crust Ingredients:** In a medium bowl, combine the graham cracker crumbs, granulated sugar, and melted butter. Mix until the crumbs are evenly coated and the mixture resembles wet sand.
   - **Press into Pan:** Press the mixture evenly into the bottom of a 9-inch (23 cm) springform pan to form the crust. Use the back of a spoon to pack it down firmly.
   - **Bake:** Bake the crust in the preheated oven for 10 minutes. Remove from the oven and let it cool while you prepare the filling.
2. **Prepare the Cheesecake Filling:**

- **Beat Cream Cheese:** In a large mixing bowl, beat the softened cream cheese with an electric mixer until smooth and creamy.
- **Add Honey and Sugar:** Gradually add the honey and granulated sugar, beating until well combined.
- **Incorporate Sour Cream and Cream:** Mix in the sour cream and heavy cream until smooth.
- **Add Eggs:** Beat in the eggs one at a time, mixing well after each addition. Add the flour and mix until just combined.
- **Flavoring:** Stir in the orange blossom water, vanilla extract, and orange zest.
- **Pour Filling:** Pour the cheesecake filling over the cooled crust in the springform pan, smoothing the top with a spatula.

3. **Bake the Cheesecake:**
   - **Prepare Water Bath:** To prevent cracking, wrap the bottom of the springform pan with aluminum foil to make it watertight. Place the pan in a large roasting pan and add hot water to the roasting pan until it comes halfway up the sides of the springform pan.
   - **Bake:** Bake the cheesecake in the preheated oven for 60-70 minutes, or until the center is set and the edges are slightly puffed but the center still has a slight jiggle.
   - **Cool Slowly:** Turn off the oven, crack the oven door slightly, and let the cheesecake cool in the oven for 1 hour. Remove from the water bath and refrigerate for at least 4 hours or overnight.

4. **Prepare the Honey Glaze (Optional):**
   - **Heat Glaze:** In a small saucepan, combine the honey and water. Heat over low heat until the honey is thinned and smooth.
   - **Cool:** Let it cool slightly before drizzling over the cheesecake.

5. **Serve:**
   - **Garnish:** Before serving, optionally drizzle the cheesecake with the honey glaze. Garnish with orange zest and fresh mint leaves.
   - **Slice and Enjoy:** Carefully remove the cheesecake from the springform pan and slice into wedges.

Tips:

- **Orange Blossom Water:** This ingredient adds a unique floral flavor. Use sparingly, as it is quite potent.
- **Avoid Cracking:** Baking the cheesecake in a water bath helps to prevent cracks and ensures even cooking.
- **Chilling:** Make sure to chill the cheesecake thoroughly for the best texture and flavor.

Enjoy your Orange Blossom and Honey Cheesecake—a sophisticated and flavorful dessert that combines floral, citrus, and sweet honey notes for a truly memorable treat!

Gingerbread Panna Cotta with Cardamom Syrup

Ingredients:

For the Gingerbread Panna Cotta:

- 1 cup (240ml) heavy cream
- 1 cup (240ml) whole milk
- 1/2 cup (100g) granulated sugar
- 1/4 cup (60ml) molasses
- 1/2 teaspoon ground ginger
- 1/2 teaspoon ground cinnamon
- 1/4 teaspoon ground cloves
- 1/4 teaspoon ground nutmeg
- 1 tablespoon (1 packet) unflavored gelatin
- 1/4 cup (60ml) cold water
- 1 teaspoon vanilla extract

For the Cardamom Syrup:

- 1 cup (200g) granulated sugar
- 1/2 cup (120ml) water
- 6 green cardamom pods, lightly crushed
- 1/2 teaspoon lemon juice

For Garnish (optional):

- Crystallized ginger, finely chopped
- Fresh mint leaves

Instructions:

1. **Prepare the Gingerbread Panna Cotta:**
   - **Bloom Gelatin:** In a small bowl, sprinkle the gelatin over the cold water and let it sit for about 5 minutes to bloom.
   - **Heat Cream Mixture:** In a medium saucepan, combine the heavy cream, whole milk, granulated sugar, molasses, ground ginger, cinnamon, cloves, and nutmeg. Heat over medium heat, stirring occasionally, until the mixture is hot but not boiling.
   - **Dissolve Gelatin:** Remove the saucepan from heat. Stir the bloomed gelatin into the hot cream mixture until completely dissolved. Stir in the vanilla extract.
   - **Cool and Set:** Pour the mixture into individual serving glasses or ramekins. Refrigerate for at least 4 hours, or until the panna cotta is set.
2. **Prepare the Cardamom Syrup:**

- **Combine Ingredients:** In a small saucepan, combine the granulated sugar, water, and crushed cardamom pods.
- **Cook Syrup:** Heat over medium heat, stirring until the sugar is completely dissolved. Bring to a simmer and cook for about 5 minutes to infuse the cardamom flavor.
- **Finish Syrup:** Remove from heat and stir in the lemon juice. Let the syrup cool to room temperature. Remove the cardamom pods before serving.

3. **Serve the Panna Cotta:**
   - **Unmold (optional):** If you prefer to unmold the panna cotta, dip the bottoms of the ramekins briefly in hot water to loosen. Invert onto serving plates.
   - **Top with Syrup:** Spoon the cardamom syrup over the panna cotta just before serving.
   - **Garnish:** Optionally, garnish with finely chopped crystallized ginger and fresh mint leaves.

Tips:

- **Gelatin:** Ensure that the gelatin is fully dissolved to avoid lumps in the panna cotta.
- **Cardamom Pods:** Lightly crush the cardamom pods to release their flavor, but be sure to strain them out before serving.
- **Serving:** The panna cotta can be made a day or two in advance, making it a convenient option for entertaining.

Enjoy your Gingerbread Panna Cotta with Cardamom Syrup—a perfect dessert to celebrate the holiday season or any occasion where a touch of warmth and spice is appreciated!

Salted Caramel Chocolate Cheesecake

Ingredients:

For the Crust:

- 1 1/2 cups (150g) chocolate cookie crumbs (such as Oreo or chocolate graham crackers)
- 1/4 cup (50g) granulated sugar
- 1/2 cup (115g) unsalted butter, melted

For the Cheesecake Filling:

- 3 (8-ounce) packages (675g total) cream cheese, softened
- 1 cup (200g) granulated sugar
- 1 cup (240ml) sour cream
- 1 cup (240ml) heavy cream
- 1 cup (180g) semi-sweet or bittersweet chocolate, chopped
- 3 large eggs
- 1 teaspoon vanilla extract
- 1/4 cup (30g) unsweetened cocoa powder

For the Salted Caramel Sauce:

- 1 cup (200g) granulated sugar
- 6 tablespoons (85g) unsalted butter, cut into pieces
- 1/2 cup (120ml) heavy cream
- 1/2 teaspoon sea salt (adjust to taste)

For Garnish:

- Whipped cream
- Additional sea salt
- Chocolate shavings or curls

Instructions:

1. **Prepare the Crust:**
    - **Preheat Oven:** Preheat your oven to 350°F (175°C). Grease and line the bottom of a 9-inch (23 cm) springform pan with parchment paper.
    - **Mix Crust Ingredients:** In a medium bowl, combine the chocolate cookie crumbs, granulated sugar, and melted butter. Mix until the crumbs are evenly coated and the mixture resembles wet sand.

- **Press into Pan:** Press the mixture evenly into the bottom of the prepared springform pan. Use the back of a spoon or the bottom of a glass to pack it down firmly.
- **Bake:** Bake the crust in the preheated oven for 10 minutes. Remove and let it cool while you prepare the filling.

2. **Prepare the Cheesecake Filling:**
   - **Melt Chocolate:** In a heatproof bowl, melt the chopped chocolate over a double boiler or in the microwave in 30-second intervals, stirring until smooth. Let it cool slightly.
   - **Beat Cream Cheese:** In a large mixing bowl, beat the softened cream cheese with an electric mixer until smooth and creamy.
   - **Add Sugar and Cocoa:** Gradually add the granulated sugar and cocoa powder, mixing until well combined.
   - **Incorporate Sour Cream and Cream:** Mix in the sour cream and heavy cream until smooth.
   - **Add Eggs and Vanilla:** Beat in the eggs one at a time, mixing well after each addition. Stir in the vanilla extract and melted chocolate until fully incorporated.
   - **Pour Filling:** Pour the cheesecake filling over the cooled crust, smoothing the top with a spatula.

3. **Bake the Cheesecake:**
   - **Prepare Water Bath:** To prevent cracks, wrap the bottom of the springform pan with aluminum foil to make it watertight. Place the pan in a large roasting pan and add hot water to the roasting pan until it comes halfway up the sides of the springform pan.
   - **Bake:** Bake the cheesecake in the preheated oven for 60-70 minutes, or until the edges are set and the center is slightly jiggly. Turn off the oven and let the cheesecake cool in the oven with the door slightly ajar for 1 hour.
   - **Chill:** Remove from the water bath and refrigerate for at least 4 hours or overnight.

4. **Prepare the Salted Caramel Sauce:**
   - **Cook Sugar:** In a medium saucepan over medium heat, cook the granulated sugar, stirring constantly, until it melts and turns a deep amber color.
   - **Add Butter:** Carefully add the butter, stirring until melted and smooth.
   - **Add Cream:** Slowly pour in the heavy cream, stirring constantly. The mixture will bubble up, so be cautious. Continue to stir until smooth.
   - **Add Sea Salt:** Remove from heat and stir in the sea salt. Let the caramel sauce cool to room temperature before using.

5. **Serve:**
   - **Top with Caramel:** Before serving, drizzle some of the salted caramel sauce over the top of the cheesecake.
   - **Garnish:** Optionally, garnish with whipped cream, a sprinkle of additional sea salt, and chocolate shavings or curls.

Tips:

- **Cooling:** Allow the cheesecake to cool completely before refrigerating to prevent condensation.
- **Caramel:** Make the caramel sauce in advance and store it in the refrigerator. Reheat slightly before drizzling over the cheesecake.
- **Serving:** For a clean slice, use a knife dipped in hot water and wiped dry between cuts.

Enjoy your Salted Caramel Chocolate Cheesecake—a rich, indulgent dessert with the perfect balance of chocolate and caramel flavors!

Pear and Almond Cake with Amaretto Glaze

Ingredients:

For the Cake:

- 1 1/2 cups (190g) all-purpose flour
- 1/2 cup (50g) almond meal (ground almonds)
- 1 1/2 teaspoons baking powder
- 1/4 teaspoon salt
- 1/2 cup (115g) unsalted butter, softened
- 1 cup (200g) granulated sugar
- 2 large eggs
- 1/2 cup (120ml) whole milk
- 1 teaspoon vanilla extract
- 1/2 teaspoon almond extract
- 2 medium ripe pears, peeled, cored, and diced

For the Amaretto Glaze:

- 1 cup (120g) powdered sugar
- 2 tablespoons amaretto liqueur
- 1-2 tablespoons milk (adjust for desired consistency)

For Garnish (optional):

- Sliced almonds
- Fresh mint leaves

Instructions:

1. **Prepare the Cake:**
    - **Preheat Oven:** Preheat your oven to 350°F (175°C). Grease and flour a 9-inch (23 cm) round cake pan or line it with parchment paper.
    - **Mix Dry Ingredients:** In a medium bowl, whisk together the all-purpose flour, almond meal, baking powder, and salt.
    - **Cream Butter and Sugar:** In a large mixing bowl, beat the softened butter and granulated sugar until light and fluffy.
    - **Add Eggs:** Beat in the eggs one at a time, mixing well after each addition.
    - **Combine Wet and Dry Ingredients:** Gradually add the dry ingredients to the butter mixture, alternating with the milk, beginning and ending with the dry ingredients. Mix until just combined. Stir in the vanilla and almond extracts.
    - **Fold in Pears:** Gently fold the diced pears into the batter.
    - **Pour into Pan:** Pour the batter into the prepared cake pan and smooth the top with a spatula.

- **Bake:** Bake in the preheated oven for 30-35 minutes, or until a toothpick inserted into the center comes out clean.
- **Cool:** Allow the cake to cool in the pan for 10 minutes, then transfer it to a wire rack to cool completely.

2. **Prepare the Amaretto Glaze:**
   - **Mix Glaze:** In a small bowl, whisk together the powdered sugar, amaretto liqueur, and 1 tablespoon of milk. Add more milk if needed to achieve a smooth, pourable consistency.
   - **Glaze Cake:** Once the cake has cooled completely, drizzle the amaretto glaze over the top, allowing it to drip down the sides.
3. **Garnish and Serve:**
   - **Garnish:** Optionally, garnish with sliced almonds and fresh mint leaves.
   - **Serve:** Slice and serve the cake at room temperature.

Tips:

- **Pears:** Choose ripe pears for the best flavor and texture. You can also use canned pears if fresh ones are not available.
- **Glaze Consistency:** Adjust the amount of milk in the glaze to reach your desired consistency. If it's too thick, add a bit more milk; if too thin, add a little more powdered sugar.
- **Storage:** The cake can be stored at room temperature for a few days. For longer storage, keep it in an airtight container in the refrigerator.

Enjoy your Pear and Almond Cake with Amaretto Glaze—a wonderfully moist and flavorful cake that pairs beautifully with coffee or tea!

Mango Sticky Rice with Coconut Sauce

Ingredients:

For the Sticky Rice:

- 1 cup (200g) glutinous (sticky) rice
- 1 1/2 cups (360ml) water
- 1/4 teaspoon salt

For the Coconut Sauce:

- 1 cup (240ml) coconut milk
- 1/4 cup (50g) granulated sugar
- 1/4 teaspoon salt
- 1 tablespoon cornstarch (optional, for thickening)

For Serving:

- 2 ripe mangoes, peeled, pitted, and sliced
- Sesame seeds or toasted coconut flakes (optional, for garnish)

Instructions:

1. **Prepare the Sticky Rice:**
   - **Rinse Rice:** Rinse the sticky rice under cold water until the water runs clear to remove excess starch.
   - **Soak:** Soak the rice in a bowl of water for at least 1 hour or overnight. Drain well.
   - **Cook Rice:** Place the soaked rice and 1 1/2 cups of water in a steamer basket lined with cheesecloth or parchment paper. Steam over boiling water for about 30-40 minutes, or until the rice is tender and translucent. If using a rice cooker, follow the manufacturer's instructions for cooking sticky rice.
   - **Season:** Once cooked, transfer the rice to a large bowl and stir in 1/4 teaspoon salt. Let it cool slightly.
2. **Prepare the Coconut Sauce:**
   - **Combine Ingredients:** In a small saucepan, combine the coconut milk, granulated sugar, and 1/4 teaspoon salt.
   - **Heat:** Heat the mixture over medium heat, stirring occasionally, until the sugar is dissolved and the mixture is warm. If using cornstarch to thicken, dissolve 1 tablespoon of cornstarch in 2 tablespoons of water and add it to the warm coconut milk, stirring constantly until the sauce thickens slightly. Remove from heat and let it cool.
3. **Assemble the Dessert:**
   - **Serve:** Place a portion of the sticky rice on individual serving plates or bowls. Arrange the mango slices on top or beside the rice.

- **Drizzle:** Drizzle the warm coconut sauce over the sticky rice and mango.
- **Garnish:** Optionally, garnish with sesame seeds or toasted coconut flakes for added texture and flavor.

Tips:

- **Mangoes:** Use ripe, sweet mangoes for the best flavor. If mangoes are not in season, you can use other tropical fruits like papaya or even canned fruit.
- **Coconut Sauce:** The coconut sauce can be made ahead of time and reheated before serving. If it thickens too much upon cooling, simply warm it up and stir before drizzling.
- **Sticky Rice:** Ensure the sticky rice is cooked through and slightly sticky for the best texture. If it's too dry, add a little bit of water and steam it again briefly.

Enjoy your Mango Sticky Rice with Coconut Sauce—a wonderfully satisfying and refreshing dessert that combines creamy, sweet, and fragrant flavors!

Cherry Clafoutis with Almond Cream

Ingredients:

For the Cherry Clafoutis:

- 2 cups (300g) fresh cherries, pitted (or use frozen, thawed and drained)
- 1 cup (240ml) whole milk
- 1/2 cup (120ml) heavy cream
- 3 large eggs
- 1/2 cup (100g) granulated sugar
- 1/4 cup (30g) all-purpose flour
- 1/4 teaspoon salt
- 1 teaspoon vanilla extract
- 1/4 teaspoon almond extract
- 2 tablespoons unsalted butter, melted (for greasing the pan)

For the Almond Cream:

- 1/2 cup (100g) almond meal (ground almonds)
- 1/4 cup (50g) granulated sugar
- 1/4 cup (60g) unsalted butter, softened
- 1 large egg
- 1/4 teaspoon almond extract

For Garnish (optional):

- Powdered sugar
- Sliced almonds
- Fresh mint leaves

Instructions:

1. **Prepare the Almond Cream:**
   - **Mix Ingredients:** In a medium bowl, combine the almond meal, granulated sugar, and softened butter. Beat in the egg and almond extract until smooth and creamy.
   - **Set Aside:** Set the almond cream aside while you prepare the clafoutis batter.
2. **Prepare the Clafoutis:**
   - **Preheat Oven:** Preheat your oven to 350°F (175°C). Grease a 9-inch (23 cm) round baking dish or pie pan with the melted butter.
   - **Arrange Cherries:** Spread the pitted cherries evenly in the bottom of the prepared baking dish.
   - **Make Batter:** In a large bowl, whisk together the milk, heavy cream, eggs, granulated sugar, flour, salt, vanilla extract, and almond extract until smooth.

- **Combine:** Pour the clafoutis batter over the cherries in the baking dish.
3. **Add Almond Cream:**
    - **Dollop Almond Cream:** Spoon dollops of the almond cream over the clafoutis batter. The almond cream will swirl into the batter as it bakes, creating a marbled effect.
4. **Bake:**
    - **Bake:** Bake in the preheated oven for 35-45 minutes, or until the clafoutis is puffed, golden brown, and set in the center. A toothpick inserted into the center should come out clean.
    - **Cool:** Allow the clafoutis to cool slightly before serving. It can be served warm or at room temperature.
5. **Garnish and Serve:**
    - **Garnish:** Optionally, dust with powdered sugar, sprinkle with sliced almonds, and garnish with fresh mint leaves.
    - **Serve:** Slice and serve the clafoutis warm or at room temperature.

Tips:

- **Cherries:** Use ripe, sweet cherries for the best flavor. If using frozen cherries, make sure they are well-drained to avoid excess moisture in the batter.
- **Almond Cream:** The almond cream adds a rich, nutty flavor to the clafoutis. For a smoother texture, you can blend the almond cream ingredients in a food processor.
- **Texture:** Clafoutis is meant to be a bit custard-like, so don't be alarmed if the center is slightly wobbly when it comes out of the oven. It will set further as it cools.

Enjoy your Cherry Clafoutis with Almond Cream—a delightful and elegant dessert that pairs wonderfully with a dollop of whipped cream or a scoop of vanilla ice cream!

Lime and Coconut Mousse with Pineapple Salsa

Ingredients:

For the Lime and Coconut Mousse:

- 1 cup (240ml) coconut milk (full-fat)
- 1 cup (240ml) heavy cream
- 1/2 cup (100g) granulated sugar
- 1/2 cup (120ml) fresh lime juice (about 4 limes)
- 1 tablespoon lime zest
- 2 large egg yolks
- 2 teaspoons unflavored gelatin
- 2 tablespoons cold water

For the Pineapple Salsa:

- 1 cup (150g) fresh pineapple, diced
- 1/4 cup (30g) red bell pepper, finely diced
- 2 tablespoons red onion, finely diced
- 1 tablespoon fresh cilantro, chopped
- 1 tablespoon fresh lime juice
- 1 teaspoon honey (optional, for sweetness)
- Pinch of salt

For Garnish (optional):

- Fresh mint leaves
- Lime wedges

Instructions:

1. **Prepare the Lime and Coconut Mousse:**
   - **Bloom Gelatin:** In a small bowl, sprinkle the gelatin over the cold water and let it sit for about 5 minutes to bloom.
   - **Heat Coconut Milk:** In a medium saucepan, combine the coconut milk and granulated sugar. Heat over medium heat, stirring occasionally, until the sugar is dissolved and the mixture is hot but not boiling.
   - **Temper Egg Yolks:** In a separate bowl, whisk the egg yolks. Gradually whisk in a small amount of the hot coconut milk mixture to temper the yolks, then pour the tempered yolks back into the saucepan.
   - **Cook Custard:** Cook the mixture over medium heat, stirring constantly, until it thickens slightly and reaches 170°F (77°C) on a thermometer. Do not let it boil.
   - **Add Gelatin and Lime:** Remove from heat and stir in the bloomed gelatin until fully dissolved. Stir in the lime juice and lime zest. Let the mixture cool to room temperature.
   - **Whip Cream:** In a large bowl, whip the heavy cream until stiff peaks form.

- **Fold Together:** Gently fold the whipped cream into the cooled coconut mixture until well combined.
- **Chill:** Spoon the mousse into serving glasses or bowls and refrigerate for at least 2 hours, or until set.

2. **Prepare the Pineapple Salsa:**
   - **Combine Ingredients:** In a medium bowl, combine the diced pineapple, red bell pepper, red onion, cilantro, lime juice, and honey (if using).
   - **Season:** Add a pinch of salt to taste. Mix well and let the salsa sit for at least 15 minutes to allow the flavors to meld.
3. **Serve:**
   - **Top Mousse:** Just before serving, top each serving of mousse with a generous spoonful of pineapple salsa.
   - **Garnish:** Optionally, garnish with fresh mint leaves and lime wedges.

Tips:

- **Coconut Milk:** For the best flavor and texture, use full-fat coconut milk. Light coconut milk can be used but may result in a less creamy mousse.
- **Gelatin:** Make sure the gelatin is completely dissolved to avoid lumps in the mousse.
- **Pineapple Salsa:** Adjust the sweetness of the salsa with honey according to your taste and the ripeness of the pineapple.

Enjoy your Lime and Coconut Mousse with Pineapple Salsa—a light, tropical dessert that's perfect for summer or any time you want a taste of paradise!

Raspberry and Rosewater Panna Cotta

Ingredients:

For the Panna Cotta:

- 1 cup (240ml) heavy cream
- 1 cup (240ml) whole milk
- 1/2 cup (100g) granulated sugar
- 1 teaspoon rosewater (adjust to taste)
- 1 teaspoon vanilla extract
- 1 tablespoon (1 packet) unflavored gelatin
- 1/4 cup (60ml) cold water

For the Raspberry Coulis:

- 1 cup (125g) fresh or frozen raspberries
- 1/4 cup (50g) granulated sugar
- 1 tablespoon fresh lemon juice

For Garnish (optional):

- Fresh raspberries
- Edible rose petals or mint leaves

Instructions:

1. **Prepare the Panna Cotta:**
   - **Bloom Gelatin:** In a small bowl, sprinkle the gelatin over the cold water and let it sit for about 5 minutes to bloom.
   - **Heat Cream Mixture:** In a medium saucepan, combine the heavy cream, whole milk, and granulated sugar. Heat over medium heat, stirring occasionally, until the sugar is completely dissolved and the mixture is hot but not boiling.
   - **Dissolve Gelatin:** Remove the saucepan from heat and stir in the bloomed gelatin until fully dissolved. Add the rosewater and vanilla extract, stirring well to combine.
   - **Cool and Pour:** Let the mixture cool slightly before pouring it into individual serving glasses or ramekins. Refrigerate for at least 4 hours, or until the panna cotta is set.
2. **Prepare the Raspberry Coulis:**
   - **Cook Raspberries:** In a small saucepan, combine the raspberries, granulated sugar, and lemon juice. Cook over medium heat, stirring occasionally, until the raspberries break down and the sauce thickens slightly (about 5-7 minutes).

- **Blend and Strain:** Puree the raspberry mixture using an immersion blender or in a regular blender until smooth. Strain through a fine-mesh sieve to remove seeds, if desired. Let the coulis cool to room temperature.
3. **Serve:**
    - **Top with Coulis:** Before serving, spoon a generous amount of raspberry coulis over each panna cotta.
    - **Garnish:** Optionally, garnish with fresh raspberries and edible rose petals or mint leaves.

Tips:

- **Rosewater:** Use rosewater sparingly as it is quite potent. Start with less and add more to taste if needed.
- **Texture:** The panna cotta should be creamy and slightly wobbly. If it's too firm, reduce the amount of gelatin slightly next time.
- **Coulis:** The raspberry coulis can be made ahead of time and stored in the refrigerator for up to a week.

Enjoy your Raspberry and Rosewater Panna Cotta—a beautifully balanced dessert with a floral touch and vibrant raspberry flavor!

Blackberry and Sage Tart

Ingredients:

For the Tart Crust:

- 1 1/4 cups (150g) all-purpose flour
- 1/4 cup (25g) powdered sugar
- 1/2 teaspoon salt
- 1/2 cup (115g) unsalted butter, cold and cut into small pieces
- 1 large egg yolk
- 2 tablespoons ice water (more if needed)

For the Blackberry Filling:

- 2 cups (300g) fresh blackberries (or frozen, thawed and drained)
- 1/2 cup (100g) granulated sugar
- 1 tablespoon cornstarch
- 1 tablespoon lemon juice
- 1 tablespoon finely chopped fresh sage leaves

For the Sage Cream:

- 1 cup (240ml) heavy cream
- 1/4 cup (50g) granulated sugar
- 1 tablespoon finely chopped fresh sage leaves
- 1/2 teaspoon vanilla extract

For Garnish (optional):

- Fresh sage leaves
- Additional blackberries

Instructions:

1. **Prepare the Tart Crust:**
    - **Mix Dry Ingredients:** In a food processor, combine the all-purpose flour, powdered sugar, and salt. Pulse to combine.
    - **Cut in Butter:** Add the cold butter pieces and pulse until the mixture resembles coarse crumbs.
    - **Add Egg Yolk and Water:** Add the egg yolk and pulse to combine. Gradually add the ice water, one tablespoon at a time, until the dough starts to come together.
    - **Chill Dough:** Transfer the dough to a lightly floured surface and shape it into a disk. Wrap in plastic wrap and refrigerate for at least 30 minutes.

2. **Preheat Oven and Prepare Tart Pan:**
   - **Preheat Oven:** Preheat your oven to 375°F (190°C).
   - **Roll Out Dough:** On a lightly floured surface, roll out the dough to fit a 9-inch (23 cm) tart pan. Gently press the dough into the pan, trimming any excess. Prick the bottom of the crust with a fork.
   - **Blind Bake:** Line the tart shell with parchment paper and fill with pie weights or dried beans. Bake for 15 minutes. Remove the parchment and weights and bake for an additional 5-7 minutes, or until the crust is golden brown. Let it cool completely.
3. **Prepare the Blackberry Filling:**
   - **Combine Ingredients:** In a medium saucepan, combine the blackberries, granulated sugar, cornstarch, lemon juice, and chopped sage. Cook over medium heat, stirring occasionally, until the mixture starts to thicken and the blackberries have softened (about 5-7 minutes). Remove from heat and let cool slightly.
   - **Fill Tart Shell:** Pour the blackberry filling into the cooled tart shell, spreading it evenly.
4. **Prepare the Sage Cream:**
   - **Heat Cream and Sage:** In a small saucepan, heat the heavy cream and chopped sage over medium heat until it just begins to simmer. Remove from heat and let it steep for 10 minutes.
   - **Strain and Sweeten:** Strain the cream through a fine-mesh sieve into a bowl, discarding the sage leaves. Stir in the granulated sugar and vanilla extract. Chill until ready to use.
5. **Serve:**
   - **Top with Sage Cream:** Before serving, spoon or drizzle the sage cream over the blackberry filling.
   - **Garnish:** Optionally, garnish with additional fresh sage leaves and blackberries.

Tips:

- **Sage Flavor:** Be cautious with the amount of sage; it should complement but not overpower the other flavors. Adjust to taste.
- **Tart Shell:** Ensure the tart shell is completely cool before adding the filling to prevent a soggy crust.
- **Storage:** The tart can be stored in the refrigerator for a few days. The sage cream should be kept separately and added just before serving.

Enjoy your Blackberry and Sage Tart—a beautifully balanced dessert that offers a delightful combination of sweet, tangy, and aromatic flavors!

Chai Spiced Poached Pears

Ingredients:

For the Poached Pears:

- 4 large firm pears (such as Bosc or Anjou), peeled, cored, and stems left intact
- 2 cups (480ml) water
- 1 cup (240ml) chai tea (brewed strong, from about 2-3 tea bags or loose-leaf)
- 1/2 cup (100g) granulated sugar
- 1/4 cup (60ml) honey
- 1 cinnamon stick
- 4-5 whole cloves
- 4-5 whole cardamom pods
- 1 star anise
- 1 teaspoon freshly grated ginger
- 1 teaspoon vanilla extract

For Garnish (optional):

- Fresh mint leaves
- Crushed pistachios or almonds
- Light drizzle of honey

Instructions:

1. **Prepare the Poaching Liquid:**
   - **Brew Chai Tea:** Brew a strong cup of chai tea and set aside.
   - **Combine Ingredients:** In a large saucepan, combine the water, chai tea, granulated sugar, honey, cinnamon stick, cloves, cardamom pods, star anise, and freshly grated ginger. Bring to a boil, stirring until the sugar is dissolved.
2. **Poach the Pears:**
   - **Add Pears:** Reduce the heat to a simmer and add the peeled and cored pears to the saucepan.
   - **Simmer:** Simmer the pears gently for 20-30 minutes, turning occasionally, until they are tender but still hold their shape. The cooking time may vary depending on the size and ripeness of the pears.
   - **Cool Pears:** Once the pears are tender, remove them from the poaching liquid and set aside to cool. Continue to simmer the poaching liquid until it reduces slightly and thickens to a syrupy consistency, about 10 minutes.
3. **Serve:**
   - **Drizzle Syrup:** Place the cooled pears on serving plates or in bowls. Drizzle with the reduced chai syrup.
   - **Garnish:** Optionally, garnish with fresh mint leaves, crushed pistachios or almonds, and a light drizzle of honey.

Tips:

- **Pear Selection:** Choose pears that are firm and slightly underripe for the best texture after poaching. They should be tender but not mushy.
- **Chai Tea:** For a more intense chai flavor, you can steep the tea bags or loose-leaf tea longer. Adjust the sweetness of the poaching liquid according to your taste.
- **Reduce Syrup:** If the syrup thickens too much while reducing, you can dilute it with a little water.

Enjoy your Chai Spiced Poached Pears—a beautifully spiced, aromatic dessert that's both comforting and sophisticated!

Tiramisu Cheesecake with Coffee Cream

Ingredients:

For the Crust:

- 1 1/2 cups (150g) graham cracker crumbs (or digestive biscuits)
- 1/4 cup (50g) granulated sugar
- 1/2 cup (115g) unsalted butter, melted

For the Cheesecake Filling:

- 16 oz (450g) cream cheese, softened
- 1 cup (240ml) heavy cream
- 1 cup (240ml) mascarpone cheese, softened
- 1 cup (200g) granulated sugar
- 3 large eggs
- 1/2 cup (120ml) strong brewed coffee, cooled
- 2 teaspoons vanilla extract
- 1/4 cup (60ml) coffee liqueur (optional, or use more brewed coffee)

For the Coffee Cream Topping:

- 1 cup (240ml) heavy cream
- 2 tablespoons powdered sugar
- 1 tablespoon strong brewed coffee or espresso, cooled
- 1 teaspoon vanilla extract

For Garnish (optional):

- Cocoa powder
- Chocolate shavings
- Coffee beans

Instructions:

1. **Prepare the Crust:**
   - **Preheat Oven:** Preheat your oven to 350°F (175°C).
   - **Mix Ingredients:** In a medium bowl, combine the graham cracker crumbs, granulated sugar, and melted butter. Mix until the crumbs are evenly coated and resemble wet sand.
   - **Press Crust:** Press the mixture firmly into the bottom of a 9-inch (23 cm) springform pan to form an even layer. Use the back of a spoon or a flat-bottomed glass to press it down firmly.
   - **Bake:** Bake the crust in the preheated oven for 8-10 minutes. Remove from the oven and let it cool slightly while you prepare the filling.
2. **Prepare the Cheesecake Filling:**

- **Beat Cream Cheese:** In a large mixing bowl, beat the softened cream cheese until smooth and creamy.
- **Add Mascarpone and Sugar:** Add the mascarpone cheese and granulated sugar, and continue to beat until well combined.
- **Add Eggs and Coffee:** Beat in the eggs one at a time, mixing well after each addition. Add the cooled coffee, vanilla extract, and coffee liqueur (if using). Mix until just combined.
- **Pour Filling:** Pour the cheesecake filling over the cooled crust in the springform pan and smooth the top with a spatula.
- **Bake:** Bake in the preheated oven for 55-65 minutes, or until the center is set and the edges are slightly puffed. The center should still have a slight jiggle when gently shaken.
- **Cool:** Turn off the oven and crack the oven door slightly. Let the cheesecake cool in the oven for 1 hour, then transfer to the refrigerator and chill for at least 4 hours or overnight.

3. **Prepare the Coffee Cream Topping:**
   - **Whip Cream:** In a medium bowl, beat the heavy cream, powdered sugar, coffee or espresso, and vanilla extract until soft peaks form.
   - **Spread Topping:** Once the cheesecake is fully chilled and set, spread the coffee cream evenly over the top of the cheesecake.
4. **Garnish and Serve:**
   - **Garnish:** Optionally, dust with cocoa powder, and sprinkle with chocolate shavings or coffee beans.
   - **Serve:** Slice and serve the cheesecake chilled.

Tips:

- **Cream Cheese:** Ensure the cream cheese and mascarpone are well-softened to avoid lumps in the filling.
- **Baking:** If you notice the cheesecake browning too quickly, cover the top loosely with foil.
- **Chilling:** For the best texture, allow the cheesecake to chill thoroughly before serving.

Enjoy your Tiramisu Cheesecake with Coffee Cream—a decadent and elegant dessert that beautifully blends the flavors of tiramisu and cheesecake!

White Chocolate and Passion Fruit Mousse

Ingredients:

For the Mousse:

- 6 oz (170g) white chocolate, chopped
- 1/2 cup (120ml) heavy cream
- 1/2 cup (120ml) passion fruit juice (fresh or store-bought)
- 1/2 cup (120ml) whole milk
- 3 large egg yolks
- 2 tablespoons granulated sugar
- 1 tablespoon unflavored gelatin
- 2 tablespoons cold water
- 1 teaspoon vanilla extract

For Garnish (optional):

- Fresh passion fruit pulp
- White chocolate shavings
- Mint leaves

Instructions:

1. **Prepare the Gelatin:**
   - **Bloom Gelatin:** In a small bowl, sprinkle the gelatin over the cold water and let it sit for about 5 minutes to bloom.
2. **Melt the White Chocolate:**
   - **Heat Cream:** In a heatproof bowl, heat the heavy cream in the microwave or over a pot of simmering water until it just begins to simmer.
   - **Melt Chocolate:** Add the chopped white chocolate to the bowl and stir until melted and smooth. Set aside.
3. **Prepare the Passion Fruit Custard:**
   - **Heat Milk:** In a saucepan, combine the whole milk and passion fruit juice. Heat over medium heat until it just begins to simmer.
   - **Whisk Egg Yolks:** In a separate bowl, whisk the egg yolks and granulated sugar until pale and slightly thickened.
   - **Temper Yolks:** Gradually whisk in a small amount of the hot milk mixture into the egg yolks to temper them. Return the egg mixture to the saucepan with the remaining milk mixture.
   - **Cook Custard:** Cook the mixture over medium heat, stirring constantly, until it thickens slightly and reaches 170°F (77°C) on a thermometer. Do not let it boil.
4. **Combine and Chill:**
   - **Dissolve Gelatin:** Remove from heat and stir in the bloomed gelatin until fully dissolved. Add the melted white chocolate and vanilla extract, stirring until well combined.
   - **Cool Mixture:** Let the mixture cool to room temperature.

5. **Whip and Fold:**
   - **Whip Cream:** In a separate bowl, whip the heavy cream until soft peaks form.
   - **Fold Together:** Gently fold the whipped cream into the cooled white chocolate and passion fruit mixture until fully combined.
6. **Chill the Mousse:**
   - **Spoon into Glasses:** Spoon the mousse into individual serving glasses or bowls.
   - **Chill:** Refrigerate for at least 4 hours, or until set.
7. **Serve:**
   - **Garnish:** Before serving, garnish with fresh passion fruit pulp, white chocolate shavings, and mint leaves if desired.

Tips:

- **Gelatin:** Make sure the gelatin is fully dissolved to avoid lumps in the mousse.
- **Passion Fruit:** If using fresh passion fruit, strain the juice to remove seeds and pulp before adding it to the custard.
- **Texture:** The mousse should be light and airy. Be gentle when folding in the whipped cream to maintain its texture.

Enjoy your White Chocolate and Passion Fruit Mousse—a beautifully balanced dessert with a rich, creamy texture and a refreshing burst of tropical flavor!

Pistachio and Rosewater Baklava

Ingredients:

For the Baklava:

- 1 package (16 oz or 450g) phyllo dough, thawed
- 1 cup (225g) unsalted butter, melted
- 2 cups (250g) shelled pistachios, finely chopped
- 1/2 cup (100g) granulated sugar
- 1 teaspoon ground cinnamon
- 1/4 teaspoon ground cardamom (optional)

For the Syrup:

- 1 cup (200g) granulated sugar
- 1/2 cup (120ml) water
- 1/4 cup (60ml) honey
- 1 tablespoon rosewater
- 1 teaspoon lemon juice

For Garnish (optional):

- Additional chopped pistachios
- Edible rose petals

Instructions:

1. **Prepare the Filling:**
   - **Mix Ingredients:** In a bowl, combine the finely chopped pistachios, granulated sugar, ground cinnamon, and ground cardamom (if using). Set aside.
2. **Prepare the Phyllo Dough:**
   - **Preheat Oven:** Preheat your oven to 350°F (175°C).
   - **Brush Phyllo:** On a clean surface, unroll the phyllo dough and cover it with a damp cloth to prevent it from drying out. Brush one sheet of phyllo with melted butter, then place another sheet on top and brush with more butter. Repeat the layering process for about 8-10 sheets.
3. **Assemble the Baklava:**
   - **Layer and Add Filling:** After the initial layers, sprinkle a thin, even layer of the pistachio mixture over the phyllo.
   - **Continue Layers:** Continue layering phyllo sheets, brushing each with melted butter, and adding the pistachio mixture every 8-10 layers. Finish with a final layer of phyllo (about 8-10 sheets), brushing each layer with butter.
   - **Cut Baklava:** Using a sharp knife, cut the baklava into diamond or square shapes, making sure to cut through all the layers.
4. **Bake the Baklava:**
   - **Bake:** Place the baklava in the preheated oven and bake for 45-50 minutes, or until the pastry is golden brown and crisp.
5. **Prepare the Syrup:**

- **Combine Ingredients:** While the baklava is baking, in a saucepan, combine the granulated sugar, water, honey, rosewater, and lemon juice. Bring to a boil, then reduce the heat and simmer for about 10 minutes, or until the syrup slightly thickens.
- **Cool Syrup:** Remove from heat and let the syrup cool to room temperature.

6. **Finish and Serve:**
   - **Pour Syrup:** Once the baklava is done baking and is still hot, pour the cooled syrup evenly over the baklava, making sure it soaks into all the cuts and layers.
   - **Cool Completely:** Allow the baklava to cool completely before serving. This allows the syrup to fully soak in and the flavors to meld.
7. **Garnish:**
   - **Optional Garnish:** Garnish with additional chopped pistachios and edible rose petals if desired.

Tips:

- **Phyllo Dough:** Keep the phyllo dough covered with a damp cloth to prevent it from drying out while working.
- **Butter:** Make sure to brush each layer of phyllo generously with melted butter to ensure a crispy, flaky texture.
- **Syrup:** The syrup should be cooled before pouring over the hot baklava to ensure it soaks in properly.

Enjoy your Pistachio and Rosewater Baklava—a luxurious and fragrant dessert that combines the traditional flavors of baklava with a delicate hint of rosewater!

Espresso Bean Chocolate Truffles

Ingredients:

For the Truffle Filling:

- 8 oz (225g) semisweet or bittersweet chocolate, chopped
- 1/2 cup (120ml) heavy cream
- 2 tablespoons unsalted butter
- 2 tablespoons finely ground espresso beans (about 2 shots of espresso)
- 1 teaspoon vanilla extract

For Coating:

- 1/2 cup (50g) cocoa powder
- 1/2 cup (50g) finely chopped chocolate (optional)
- 1/4 cup (25g) finely ground espresso beans (optional)

Instructions:

1. **Prepare the Truffle Filling:**
   - **Heat Cream:** In a small saucepan, heat the heavy cream over medium heat until it begins to simmer. Do not let it boil.
   - **Combine Ingredients:** Place the chopped chocolate and unsalted butter in a heatproof bowl. Pour the hot cream over the chocolate and butter. Let sit for about 1-2 minutes to melt, then stir until smooth and completely combined.
   - **Add Espresso and Vanilla:** Stir in the finely ground espresso beans and vanilla extract until well mixed. The mixture should be smooth and glossy.
2. **Chill the Mixture:**
   - **Cool:** Allow the truffle mixture to cool to room temperature. Once cooled, cover the bowl with plastic wrap and refrigerate for at least 2 hours, or until firm enough to scoop.
3. **Form the Truffles:**
   - **Scoop and Shape:** Using a small melon baller or a spoon, scoop out small portions of the chilled mixture and roll them into balls. If the mixture is too soft to roll, chill it for an additional 30 minutes.
   - **Chill Again:** Place the rolled truffles on a parchment-lined tray and refrigerate for about 30 minutes to set.
4. **Coat the Truffles:**
   - **Prepare Coatings:** If using cocoa powder, place it in a shallow dish. For additional coating options, you can also use finely chopped chocolate or additional finely ground espresso beans.
   - **Coat Truffles:** Roll each truffle in the cocoa powder or chosen coating until fully covered. You can also dip the truffles in melted chocolate and then coat them with cocoa powder or espresso beans for an extra layer of flavor and texture.
5. **Store and Serve:**
   - **Store:** Store the truffles in an airtight container in the refrigerator for up to 2 weeks. They can also be frozen for longer storage.

- **Serve:** Allow the truffles to come to room temperature for about 10-15 minutes before serving for the best flavor and texture.

Tips:

- **Chocolate Quality:** Use high-quality chocolate for the best flavor and texture.
- **Espresso Beans:** Adjust the amount of finely ground espresso beans to taste. You can use more or less depending on how strong you want the coffee flavor to be.
- **Coating Options:** Feel free to experiment with different coatings, such as crushed nuts or sprinkles, for added variety.

Enjoy your Espresso Bean Chocolate Truffles—a luxurious treat that combines the rich flavors of chocolate and espresso for an irresistible indulgence!

Pineapple Upside-Down Cake with Rum Glaze

Ingredients:

For the Pineapple Topping:

- 1/4 cup (60g) unsalted butter
- 1 cup (200g) brown sugar, packed
- 8-10 pineapple rings (canned or fresh)
- Maraschino cherries or fresh cherries, pitted (about 8-10)

For the Cake:

- 1 1/2 cups (190g) all-purpose flour
- 1 1/2 teaspoons baking powder
- 1/2 teaspoon salt
- 1/2 cup (115g) unsalted butter, softened
- 1 cup (200g) granulated sugar
- 2 large eggs
- 1 teaspoon vanilla extract
- 1/2 cup (120ml) milk
- 1/4 cup (60ml) pineapple juice (from canned pineapple or fresh)

For the Rum Glaze:

- 1/4 cup (60ml) dark rum
- 1/4 cup (60ml) pineapple juice
- 1/4 cup (50g) granulated sugar
- 2 tablespoons unsalted butter

Instructions:

1. **Prepare the Pineapple Topping:**
   - **Preheat Oven:** Preheat your oven to 350°F (175°C).
   - **Make Caramel:** In a medium saucepan, melt the 1/4 cup butter over medium heat. Stir in the brown sugar and cook for 2-3 minutes, until the mixture is smooth and bubbly.
   - **Arrange Pineapple:** Pour the caramel mixture into the bottom of a 9-inch (23 cm) round cake pan, spreading it evenly. Arrange the pineapple rings on top of the caramel and place a cherry in the center of each pineapple ring.
2. **Prepare the Cake Batter:**
   - **Mix Dry Ingredients:** In a medium bowl, whisk together the flour, baking powder, and salt.
   - **Cream Butter and Sugar:** In a large bowl, cream the softened butter and granulated sugar together until light and fluffy. Beat in the eggs one at a time, then add the vanilla extract.
   - **Combine Ingredients:** Gradually add the dry ingredients to the butter mixture, alternating with the milk and pineapple juice. Begin and end with the dry ingredients, mixing until just combined.
   - **Pour Batter:** Gently pour the batter over the pineapple and caramel in the cake pan, spreading it evenly.

3. **Bake the Cake:**
   - **Bake:** Bake in the preheated oven for 35-40 minutes, or until a toothpick inserted into the center comes out clean and the cake is golden brown.
   - **Cool Slightly:** Let the cake cool in the pan for about 10 minutes, then run a knife around the edges to loosen it. Carefully invert the cake onto a serving plate.
4. **Prepare the Rum Glaze:**
   - **Combine Ingredients:** In a small saucepan, combine the dark rum, pineapple juice, granulated sugar, and butter. Heat over medium heat, stirring until the sugar is dissolved and the mixture is smooth.
   - **Simmer:** Bring the glaze to a simmer and cook for about 5 minutes, or until slightly thickened.
5. **Glaze and Serve:**
   - **Drizzle Glaze:** Brush the warm rum glaze over the top of the cooled cake, allowing it to soak into the pineapple and cake.
   - **Serve:** Slice and serve the cake at room temperature. It can be enjoyed on its own or with a dollop of whipped cream or a scoop of vanilla ice cream.

Tips:

- **Pineapple:** Use canned pineapple rings for convenience, or fresh pineapple if you prefer. If using fresh pineapple, you may need to adjust the cooking time.
- **Rum Glaze:** For a non-alcoholic version, you can substitute the rum with additional pineapple juice.
- **Cake Pan:** Make sure to use a pan with high sides to prevent any caramel overflow during baking.

Enjoy your Pineapple Upside-Down Cake with Rum Glaze—a delightful combination of sweet, tangy pineapple and rich, buttery cake with a hint of rum for a tropical twist!

Chocolaty Chestnut Mousse Cake

Ingredients:

For the Chocolate Sponge Cake:

- 1/2 cup (60g) all-purpose flour

- 1/2 cup (50g) unsweetened cocoa powder
- 1/2 teaspoon baking powder
- 1/4 teaspoon salt
- 1/2 cup (115g) unsalted butter, softened
- 1/2 cup (100g) granulated sugar
- 2 large eggs
- 1/2 teaspoon vanilla extract
- 1/4 cup (60ml) whole milk

For the Chestnut Mousse:

- 1 cup (240ml) heavy cream
- 1 cup (250g) chestnut purée (canned or homemade)
- 1/2 cup (100g) granulated sugar
- 1/2 teaspoon vanilla extract
- 1 tablespoon unflavored gelatin
- 2 tablespoons cold water
- 1/2 cup (120ml) milk

For the Chocolate Glaze:

- 1/2 cup (120ml) heavy cream
- 4 oz (115g) semisweet or bittersweet chocolate, chopped
- 2 tablespoons light corn syrup

For Garnish (optional):

- Whipped cream
- Shaved chocolate
- Chestnut pieces or purée

Instructions:

1. **Prepare the Chocolate Sponge Cake:**
   - **Preheat Oven:** Preheat your oven to 350°F (175°C). Grease and line an 8-inch (20 cm) round cake pan with parchment paper.
   - **Mix Dry Ingredients:** In a medium bowl, sift together the flour, cocoa powder, baking powder, and salt.
   - **Cream Butter and Sugar:** In a large bowl, cream the softened butter and granulated sugar until light and fluffy.
   - **Add Eggs and Vanilla:** Beat in the eggs one at a time, then add the vanilla extract.
   - **Combine Ingredients:** Gradually add the dry ingredients to the butter mixture, alternating with the milk. Mix until just combined.
   - **Bake:** Pour the batter into the prepared cake pan and smooth the top. Bake for 20-25 minutes, or until a toothpick inserted into the center comes out clean. Let

the cake cool in the pan for 10 minutes, then transfer to a wire rack to cool completely.
2. **Prepare the Chestnut Mousse:**
   - **Bloom Gelatin:** In a small bowl, sprinkle the gelatin over the cold water and let it bloom for about 5 minutes.
   - **Heat Milk:** In a small saucepan, heat the milk until warm but not boiling. Remove from heat and stir in the bloomed gelatin until fully dissolved. Let cool slightly.
   - **Whip Cream:** In a medium bowl, whip the heavy cream until soft peaks form.
   - **Combine Ingredients:** In a separate bowl, mix the chestnut purée, granulated sugar, and vanilla extract until smooth. Gently fold in the whipped cream.
   - **Add Gelatin:** Fold in the gelatin mixture until fully combined.
3. **Assemble the Cake:**
   - **Prepare Mold:** Place the cooled chocolate sponge cake in the center of an 8-inch (20 cm) springform pan or cake ring lined with acetate strips.
   - **Add Mousse:** Pour the chestnut mousse over the sponge cake, spreading it evenly. Smooth the top with a spatula.
   - **Chill:** Refrigerate the cake for at least 4 hours or until the mousse is fully set.
4. **Prepare the Chocolate Glaze:**
   - **Heat Cream:** In a small saucepan, heat the heavy cream until it just begins to simmer. Remove from heat.
   - **Add Chocolate:** Add the chopped chocolate and corn syrup to the cream. Let sit for 2 minutes, then stir until smooth and glossy.
   - **Cool Slightly:** Allow the glaze to cool slightly before using.
5. **Glaze and Garnish:**
   - **Apply Glaze:** Pour the chocolate glaze over the set chestnut mousse, spreading it evenly with a spatula. Let the excess drip off.
   - **Chill Again:** Refrigerate the cake for another 30 minutes to set the glaze.
   - **Garnish:** Optionally, garnish with whipped cream, shaved chocolate, and chestnut pieces or purée before serving.

Tips:

- **Chestnut Purée:** If using canned chestnut purée, make sure it is smooth and unsweetened for the best flavor.
- **Gelatin:** Ensure the gelatin is completely dissolved to avoid lumps in the mousse.
- **Serving:** Let the cake sit at room temperature for about 10 minutes before serving to soften the mousse slightly.

Enjoy your Chocolaty Chestnut Mousse Cake—a luxurious dessert with a perfect blend of rich chocolate and creamy chestnut flavors!

Apple Cinnamon Bread Pudding with Bourbon Sauce

Ingredients:

For the Bread Pudding:

- 6 cups (about 10-12 slices) day-old bread, cubed (preferably French or Italian bread)
- 2 cups (480ml) whole milk
- 1 cup (240ml) heavy cream

- 3 large eggs
- 1 cup (200g) granulated sugar
- 1 teaspoon vanilla extract
- 1 teaspoon ground cinnamon
- 1/2 teaspoon ground nutmeg
- 2 cups (2-3 medium) apples, peeled, cored, and diced
- 1/2 cup (80g) raisins or sultanas (optional)
- 1/4 cup (60g) unsalted butter, melted

For the Bourbon Sauce:

- 1/2 cup (120ml) heavy cream
- 1/2 cup (120ml) bourbon
- 1/2 cup (100g) granulated sugar
- 2 tablespoons unsalted butter

Instructions:

1. **Prepare the Bread Pudding:**
   - **Preheat Oven:** Preheat your oven to 350°F (175°C). Grease a 9x13-inch (23x33 cm) baking dish or similar-sized dish.
   - **Soak Bread:** In a large bowl, combine the cubed bread with the milk and heavy cream. Let it sit for about 10-15 minutes, stirring occasionally, until the bread is softened and soaked.
   - **Mix Ingredients:** In a separate bowl, whisk together the eggs, granulated sugar, vanilla extract, ground cinnamon, and ground nutmeg. Stir this mixture into the soaked bread.
   - **Add Apples and Raisins:** Gently fold in the diced apples, raisins (if using), and melted butter until evenly combined.
   - **Bake:** Pour the bread mixture into the prepared baking dish and spread it evenly. Bake in the preheated oven for 45-55 minutes, or until the pudding is set in the center and the top is golden brown. A knife inserted into the center should come out clean.
2. **Prepare the Bourbon Sauce:**
   - **Combine Ingredients:** In a medium saucepan, combine the heavy cream, bourbon, granulated sugar, and unsalted butter.
   - **Heat and Stir:** Heat over medium heat, stirring constantly until the sugar is fully dissolved and the mixture is smooth.
   - **Simmer:** Bring the mixture to a gentle simmer and cook for about 5 minutes, or until slightly thickened. Remove from heat and let it cool slightly before serving.
3. **Serve:**
   - **Spoon and Sauce:** Serve the warm bread pudding in individual portions, drizzled with the bourbon sauce.

Tips:

- **Bread:** Using slightly stale or day-old bread is ideal for this recipe, as it absorbs the custard mixture better. Fresh bread might become too mushy.
- **Apples:** Choose a firm variety of apple that holds its shape during baking, such as Honeycrisp or Granny Smith.
- **Bourbon Sauce:** Adjust the amount of bourbon to taste. If you prefer a non-alcoholic version, you can substitute the bourbon with additional milk or a splash of vanilla extract.

Enjoy your Apple Cinnamon Bread Pudding with Bourbon Sauce—a deliciously comforting dessert perfect for any occasion!

Maple Pecan Pie with Bourbon Cream

Ingredients:

For the Pie Crust:

- 1 1/2 cups (190g) all-purpose flour
- 1/2 cup (115g) unsalted butter, cold and cut into small pieces
- 1/4 cup (50g) granulated sugar
- 1/4 teaspoon salt
- 1/4 cup (60ml) ice water (more if needed)

For the Maple Pecan Filling:

- 1 cup (240ml) pure maple syrup
- 1/2 cup (100g) packed light brown sugar
- 1/2 cup (115g) unsalted butter, melted
- 3 large eggs
- 1 teaspoon vanilla extract
- 1/4 teaspoon salt
- 1 1/2 cups (150g) pecan halves

For the Bourbon Cream:

- 1 cup (240ml) heavy cream
- 2 tablespoons granulated sugar
- 1 tablespoon bourbon
- 1 teaspoon vanilla extract

Instructions:

1. **Prepare the Pie Crust:**
    - **Mix Ingredients:** In a food processor, combine the flour, granulated sugar, and salt. Add the cold butter pieces and pulse until the mixture resembles coarse crumbs.
    - **Add Water:** Gradually add the ice water, one tablespoon at a time, and pulse until the dough begins to come together. You may need a bit more water depending on your flour.
    - **Chill Dough:** Turn the dough out onto a lightly floured surface, form it into a disc, and wrap in plastic wrap. Refrigerate for at least 30 minutes.
2. **Prepare the Filling:**
    - **Preheat Oven:** Preheat your oven to 350°F (175°C).
    - **Mix Filling:** In a large bowl, whisk together the maple syrup, brown sugar, melted butter, eggs, vanilla extract, and salt until smooth.
    - **Add Pecans:** Stir in the pecan halves until well coated.
3. **Assemble the Pie:**
    - **Roll Out Dough:** On a lightly floured surface, roll out the chilled dough to fit a 9-inch (23 cm) pie dish. Transfer the dough to the dish and trim the edges, crimping them as desired.
    - **Pre-Bake Crust (optional):** For a crisper crust, pre-bake the crust: line it with parchment paper, fill with pie weights, and bake for 10 minutes. Remove the parchment and weights and bake for an additional 5 minutes. Let cool slightly.
    - **Fill Pie:** Pour the maple pecan filling into the prepared crust.
    - **Bake:** Bake in the preheated oven for 50-60 minutes, or until the filling is set and the crust is golden brown. The center should be slightly jiggly but not liquid. If the crust edges start to brown too quickly, cover them with foil.
4. **Prepare the Bourbon Cream:**

- **Whip Cream:** In a mixing bowl, combine the heavy cream and granulated sugar. Whip with an electric mixer until soft peaks form.
        - **Add Bourbon and Vanilla:** Gently fold in the bourbon and vanilla extract until combined.
5. **Serve:**
    - **Cool Pie:** Allow the pie to cool completely on a wire rack before serving. This allows the filling to set properly.
    - **Top and Garnish:** Serve each slice of pie with a dollop of bourbon cream. Optionally, garnish with additional pecans or a drizzle of maple syrup.

Tips:

- **Pecans:** Toast the pecans lightly before adding them to the filling for extra flavor.
- **Pie Crust:** If the dough is too crumbly, add a little more ice water. If it's too sticky, add a bit more flour.
- **Bourbon Cream:** For a non-alcoholic version, simply omit the bourbon and use vanilla extract instead.

Enjoy your Maple Pecan Pie with Bourbon Cream—a decadent treat that brings together the rich flavors of maple, pecans, and bourbon for a truly indulgent dessert!

Cardamom and Saffron Rice Pudding

Ingredients:

For the Rice Pudding:

- 1/2 cup (100g) short-grain or medium-grain rice (e.g., Arborio or sushi rice)
- 2 cups (480ml) whole milk
- 1 cup (240ml) heavy cream
- 1/2 cup (100g) granulated sugar
- 1/4 teaspoon ground cardamom

- 1/4 teaspoon saffron threads (about a small pinch)
- 1/2 teaspoon vanilla extract
- 1/4 teaspoon salt

For Garnish (optional):

- Chopped pistachios or almonds
- Dried rose petals
- Fresh berries or fruit slices

Instructions:

1. **Prepare the Rice:**
   - **Rinse Rice:** Rinse the rice under cold water until the water runs clear. This removes excess starch and helps achieve a creamy texture.
2. **Cook the Pudding:**
   - **Simmer Rice:** In a medium saucepan, combine the rinsed rice, milk, and heavy cream. Bring to a gentle simmer over medium heat, stirring frequently to prevent sticking.
   - **Add Saffron:** Soak the saffron threads in a small amount of warm milk or water to release their color and flavor. Stir the saffron into the rice mixture.
   - **Cook:** Reduce the heat to low and cook the mixture, stirring occasionally, for about 25-30 minutes, or until the rice is tender and the pudding has thickened to a creamy consistency.
3. **Flavor and Sweeten:**
   - **Add Cardamom and Vanilla:** Stir in the granulated sugar, ground cardamom, vanilla extract, and salt. Continue to cook for another 5 minutes, stirring, until the sugar is fully dissolved and the flavors are well combined.
   - **Adjust Consistency:** If the pudding is too thick, you can stir in a little more milk or cream to reach your desired consistency.
4. **Cool and Serve:**
   - **Cool Slightly:** Remove the saucepan from heat and let the pudding cool slightly. The pudding will continue to thicken as it cools.
   - **Serve:** Spoon the rice pudding into individual bowls or ramekins. Garnish with chopped pistachios, dried rose petals, or fresh berries if desired.
5. **Optional: Chill:**
   - **Chill:** For a colder serving option, refrigerate the pudding for at least 2 hours before serving.

Tips:

- **Rice Choice:** Short-grain or medium-grain rice is preferred for its creamy texture. Avoid using long-grain rice, which may not become as creamy.
- **Saffron:** Saffron is potent and should be used sparingly. Soaking it in warm liquid helps release its color and flavor.

- **Consistency:** Rice pudding can be served warm or cold, depending on your preference. It will thicken further upon chilling, so adjust the consistency with additional milk or cream as needed.

Enjoy your Cardamom and Saffron Rice Pudding—a beautifully fragrant and creamy dessert that's sure to delight with its exotic flavors!

Black Sesame and Ginger Ice Cream

Ingredients:

For the Ice Cream Base:

- 1 cup (240ml) whole milk
- 1 cup (240ml) heavy cream
- 3/4 cup (150g) granulated sugar
- 1/2 cup (50g) black sesame seeds, toasted and ground
- 1 tablespoon freshly grated ginger

- 4 large egg yolks
- 1 teaspoon vanilla extract
- Pinch of salt

For Garnish (optional):

- Toasted black sesame seeds
- Fresh ginger slices

Instructions:

1. **Prepare the Sesame Seeds:**
    - **Toast and Grind:** Toast the black sesame seeds in a dry skillet over medium heat until fragrant, about 2-3 minutes. Let them cool, then grind into a fine powder using a spice grinder or mortar and pestle.
2. **Make the Ice Cream Base:**
    - **Heat Milk and Cream:** In a medium saucepan, combine the whole milk, heavy cream, and granulated sugar. Heat over medium heat, stirring occasionally, until the mixture is warm and the sugar is dissolved. Do not let it boil.
    - **Add Sesame and Ginger:** Stir in the ground black sesame seeds and freshly grated ginger. Continue to heat the mixture until it is hot but not boiling.
    - **Prepare Egg Yolks:** In a separate bowl, whisk the egg yolks. Gradually ladle some of the hot milk mixture into the egg yolks while whisking to temper them.
    - **Combine Mixtures:** Pour the tempered egg yolk mixture back into the saucepan with the remaining milk mixture. Cook over medium-low heat, stirring constantly, until the mixture thickens and coats the back of a spoon (about 5-7 minutes). Do not let it boil.
    - **Strain and Cool:** Remove from heat and strain the custard through a fine-mesh sieve into a clean bowl to remove any curdled bits. Stir in the vanilla extract and a pinch of salt. Let the mixture cool to room temperature.
3. **Chill and Churn:**
    - **Chill:** Cover the bowl with plastic wrap and refrigerate the custard for at least 4 hours or overnight, until completely chilled.
    - **Churn:** Pour the chilled mixture into an ice cream maker and churn according to the manufacturer's instructions until it reaches a soft-serve consistency.
4. **Freeze:**
    - **Transfer and Freeze:** Transfer the churned ice cream to an airtight container and freeze for at least 2 hours, or until firm.
5. **Serve:**
    - **Scoop and Garnish:** Scoop the ice cream into bowls or cones. Garnish with toasted black sesame seeds and fresh ginger slices if desired.

Tips:

- **Black Sesame:** The flavor of black sesame can be quite intense. Adjust the amount to your taste preference if needed.
- **Ginger:** Use freshly grated ginger for the best flavor. If you prefer a milder ginger flavor, you can reduce the amount used.
- **Churning:** Make sure the ice cream mixture is well-chilled before churning for the best texture.

Enjoy your Black Sesame and Ginger Ice Cream—a sophisticated and flavorful treat that combines the unique taste of black sesame with the zesty warmth of ginger!

Mango Coconut Chia Pudding

Ingredients:

For the Chia Pudding:

- 1/4 cup (40g) chia seeds
- 1 cup (240ml) coconut milk (full-fat or light)
- 1/2 cup (120ml) almond milk or another plant-based milk
- 2 tablespoons maple syrup or honey (adjust to taste)

- 1/2 teaspoon vanilla extract

For the Mango Topping:

- 1 ripe mango, peeled, pitted, and diced
- 1 tablespoon lime juice
- 1 tablespoon honey or maple syrup (optional, depending on mango sweetness)

For Garnish (optional):

- Fresh mint leaves
- Shredded coconut
- Chopped nuts (e.g., almonds or cashews)

Instructions:

1. **Prepare the Chia Pudding:**
   - **Combine Ingredients:** In a medium bowl, whisk together the chia seeds, coconut milk, almond milk, maple syrup (or honey), and vanilla extract.
   - **Mix Well:** Stir the mixture well to ensure the chia seeds are evenly distributed and not clumping together.
   - **Refrigerate:** Cover the bowl and refrigerate for at least 4 hours or overnight, allowing the chia seeds to absorb the liquid and thicken into a pudding-like consistency. Stir once or twice during the first hour to prevent clumping.
2. **Prepare the Mango Topping:**
   - **Mix Mango:** In a small bowl, combine the diced mango with lime juice. If the mango is not sweet enough, you can add honey or maple syrup to taste. Let it sit for about 10 minutes to allow the flavors to meld.
3. **Assemble and Serve:**
   - **Layer Pudding and Mango:** Spoon the chia pudding into individual serving glasses or bowls. Top with the mango mixture.
   - **Garnish:** Optionally, garnish with fresh mint leaves, shredded coconut, or chopped nuts for added texture and flavor.

Tips:

- **Chia Seeds:** Make sure to stir the chia mixture a few times during the first hour of refrigeration to ensure even distribution and prevent clumping.
- **Mango:** Choose ripe mangoes for the best flavor. If mangoes are out of season, you can use frozen mango chunks that have been thawed.
- **Sweetness:** Adjust the sweetness of both the chia pudding and the mango topping according to your taste preference.

Enjoy your Mango Coconut Chia Pudding—a deliciously creamy and tropical dessert that's both healthy and satisfying!

Lavender Honey Cheesecake

Ingredients:

For the Crust:

- 1 1/2 cups (150g) graham cracker crumbs
- 1/4 cup (50g) granulated sugar
- 1/2 cup (115g) unsalted butter, melted

For the Cheesecake Filling:

- 4 (8 oz) (225g each) packages cream cheese, softened
- 1 cup (240ml) sour cream
- 1 cup (240ml) heavy cream
- 1 cup (200g) granulated sugar
- 1/2 cup (120ml) honey
- 4 large eggs
- 1 tablespoon dried lavender buds
- 1 teaspoon vanilla extract
- 1 tablespoon all-purpose flour
- Pinch of salt

For the Lavender Honey Topping:

- 1/2 cup (120ml) honey
- 1 tablespoon dried lavender buds

Instructions:

1. **Prepare the Crust:**
   - **Preheat Oven:** Preheat your oven to 325°F (160°C). Grease the sides of a 9-inch (23 cm) springform pan and line the bottom with parchment paper.
   - **Mix Crust Ingredients:** In a medium bowl, combine the graham cracker crumbs, granulated sugar, and melted butter. Mix until the crumbs are evenly coated and resemble wet sand.
   - **Press Crust:** Press the crumb mixture into the bottom of the prepared springform pan, pressing firmly to form an even layer. Bake for 10 minutes, then let cool.
2. **Prepare the Cheesecake Filling:**
   - **Infuse Cream:** In a small saucepan, heat the heavy cream over low heat until warm. Add the dried lavender buds and let steep for 10 minutes. Strain out the lavender and let the cream cool slightly.
   - **Beat Cream Cheese:** In a large mixing bowl, beat the softened cream cheese until smooth and creamy.
   - **Add Sugar and Honey:** Gradually add the granulated sugar and honey, beating until well combined.
   - **Add Eggs:** Beat in the eggs one at a time, mixing well after each addition.
   - **Incorporate Ingredients:** Add the sour cream, vanilla extract, flour, and a pinch of salt. Mix until smooth.
   - **Add Infused Cream:** Stir in the lavender-infused cream until well combined.
3. **Bake the Cheesecake:**
   - **Pour Filling:** Pour the cheesecake filling over the cooled crust in the springform pan.

- **Bake:** Bake in the preheated oven for 55-65 minutes, or until the center is set but still slightly jiggly. The edges should be firm and the center will continue to firm up as it cools.
- **Cool:** Turn off the oven and crack the oven door slightly. Let the cheesecake cool in the oven for 1 hour. Remove from the oven and let cool to room temperature. Chill in the refrigerator for at least 4 hours or overnight.

4. **Prepare the Lavender Honey Topping:**
    - **Heat Honey:** In a small saucepan, heat the honey over low heat until warm. Add the dried lavender buds and let steep for 10 minutes. Strain out the lavender buds before using.
5. **Serve:**
    - **Top Cheesecake:** Before serving, drizzle the lavender honey topping over the chilled cheesecake.
    - **Garnish (optional):** Garnish with additional dried lavender buds if desired.

Tips:

- **Lavender:** Make sure to use culinary-grade lavender for this recipe. Avoid using lavender that is meant for decorative purposes.
- **Cheesecake Texture:** To prevent cracks, bake the cheesecake in a water bath. Wrap the outside of the springform pan with aluminum foil to prevent leaks, and place it in a larger baking dish filled with hot water during baking.
- **Sweetness:** Adjust the amount of honey to taste if you prefer a sweeter or less sweet cheesecake.

Enjoy your Lavender Honey Cheesecake—a beautifully fragrant and creamy dessert that combines the elegance of lavender with the richness of honey!

Plum and Almond Frangipane Tart

Ingredients:

For the Tart Crust:

- 1 1/2 cups (190g) all-purpose flour
- 1/4 cup (50g) granulated sugar

- 1/2 teaspoon salt
- 1/2 cup (115g) unsalted butter, cold and cut into small pieces
- 1 large egg yolk
- 2-3 tablespoons ice water (as needed)

For the Frangipane Filling:

- 1/2 cup (115g) unsalted butter, softened
- 1/2 cup (100g) granulated sugar
- 1 cup (100g) almond meal or ground almonds
- 2 large eggs
- 1 teaspoon vanilla extract
- 1 tablespoon all-purpose flour
- 1/4 teaspoon salt

For the Plum Topping:

- 4-5 ripe plums, pitted and sliced
- 2 tablespoons granulated sugar
- 1 tablespoon lemon juice

For Garnish (optional):

- Powdered sugar
- Fresh mint leaves

Instructions:

1. **Prepare the Tart Crust:**
   - **Mix Dry Ingredients:** In a food processor, combine the flour, granulated sugar, and salt. Pulse briefly to mix.
   - **Cut in Butter:** Add the cold butter pieces and pulse until the mixture resembles coarse crumbs.
   - **Add Egg Yolk:** Add the egg yolk and pulse until combined.
   - **Add Water:** Gradually add ice water, one tablespoon at a time, until the dough comes together. Do not overwork the dough.
   - **Chill Dough:** Turn the dough out onto a lightly floured surface, form it into a disk, wrap in plastic wrap, and refrigerate for at least 30 minutes.
2. **Prepare the Frangipane Filling:**
   - **Cream Butter and Sugar:** In a large bowl, beat the softened butter and granulated sugar until light and fluffy.
   - **Add Almonds and Eggs:** Mix in the almond meal or ground almonds, then beat in the eggs one at a time, followed by the vanilla extract.
   - **Incorporate Flour and Salt:** Add the flour and salt, and mix until smooth.
3. **Prepare the Plum Topping:**

- **Prepare Plums:** In a small bowl, toss the sliced plums with granulated sugar and lemon juice. Set aside.
4. **Assemble the Tart:**
    - **Preheat Oven:** Preheat your oven to 375°F (190°C). Grease a 9-inch (23 cm) tart pan with removable bottom.
    - **Roll Out Dough:** On a lightly floured surface, roll out the chilled dough to fit the tart pan. Transfer the dough to the pan, pressing it into the bottom and sides. Trim any excess dough.
    - **Pre-Bake Crust (optional):** For a crisper base, pre-bake the crust: line it with parchment paper, fill with pie weights, and bake for 10 minutes. Remove the parchment and weights and bake for an additional 5 minutes. Let cool slightly.
    - **Fill Tart:** Spread the frangipane filling evenly over the pre-baked tart crust.
    - **Arrange Plums:** Arrange the plum slices on top of the frangipane filling in a decorative pattern.
5. **Bake the Tart:**
    - **Bake:** Bake in the preheated oven for 35-40 minutes, or until the frangipane is set and golden brown, and the plums are tender.
    - **Cool:** Allow the tart to cool in the pan for 10 minutes, then remove from the pan and let cool completely on a wire rack.
6. **Serve:**
    - **Garnish and Serve:** Before serving, you can dust the tart with powdered sugar and garnish with fresh mint leaves if desired.

Tips:

- **Tart Crust:** If the dough is too soft to roll out, refrigerate it for another 10-15 minutes.
- **Plum Variety:** Use ripe plums for the best flavor. You can also use other stone fruits like peaches or apricots.
- **Frangipane Texture:** The frangipane should be smooth and creamy. If it appears too thick, you can add a bit more butter or an extra egg.

Enjoy your Plum and Almond Frangipane Tart—a delightful dessert with a rich almond filling and sweet, juicy plums that's sure to impress!

Spiced Chocolate Soufflé with Vanilla Cream

Ingredients:

For the Soufflé:

- 4 tablespoons (60g) unsalted butter, plus extra for greasing
- 1/2 cup (100g) granulated sugar, plus extra for coating ramekins

- 4 oz (115g) high-quality dark chocolate (70% cocoa), chopped
- 2 large egg yolks
- 1 teaspoon ground cinnamon
- 1/4 teaspoon ground nutmeg
- 1/4 teaspoon ground allspice
- 1/4 teaspoon salt
- 4 large egg whites
- 1/4 teaspoon cream of tartar

For the Vanilla Cream:

- 1 cup (240ml) heavy cream
- 2 tablespoons granulated sugar
- 1 teaspoon vanilla extract

Instructions:

1. **Prepare the Soufflé Ramekins:**
   - **Preheat Oven:** Preheat your oven to 375°F (190°C). Place a baking sheet on the middle rack of the oven.
   - **Grease Ramekins:** Generously grease four 6-ounce (180ml) ramekins with butter. Dust the insides with granulated sugar, tapping out any excess.
2. **Make the Chocolate Mixture:**
   - **Melt Chocolate:** In a heatproof bowl set over a pot of simmering water (double boiler), melt the chopped dark chocolate, stirring occasionally until smooth. Remove from heat and let cool slightly.
   - **Mix Egg Yolks:** In a separate bowl, whisk together the egg yolks, cinnamon, nutmeg, allspice, and salt. Add the melted chocolate and mix until smooth.
3. **Prepare the Soufflé Base:**
   - **Whip Egg Whites:** In a clean, dry bowl, beat the egg whites with a hand mixer or stand mixer until foamy. Add the cream of tartar and continue to beat until soft peaks form. Gradually add the granulated sugar, beating until stiff peaks form.
   - **Fold in Chocolate Mixture:** Gently fold the whipped egg whites into the chocolate mixture in thirds, being careful not to deflate the mixture.
4. **Bake the Soufflés:**
   - **Fill Ramekins:** Spoon the soufflé mixture into the prepared ramekins, filling them almost to the top. Smooth the tops with a spatula.
   - **Bake:** Place the ramekins on the baking sheet in the oven and bake for 15-18 minutes, or until the soufflés are puffed and set. Do not open the oven door during baking.
5. **Prepare the Vanilla Cream:**
   - **Whip Cream:** In a mixing bowl, combine the heavy cream, granulated sugar, and vanilla extract. Whip with an electric mixer until soft peaks form.
   - **Serve:** Spoon or pipe the vanilla cream over or alongside the soufflés.
6. **Serve Immediately:**

- **Garnish and Serve:** Dust the tops of the soufflés with powdered sugar if desired. Serve immediately, as soufflés are best enjoyed fresh from the oven.

Tips:

- **Egg Whites:** Ensure that no yolk gets into the egg whites, as any fat can prevent them from whipping properly.
- **Soufflé Timing:** The soufflés should be served immediately after baking to enjoy their full puffiness and airy texture.
- **Preparation:** You can prepare the soufflé base in advance and store it in the refrigerator. However, the soufflés should be baked just before serving.

Enjoy your Spiced Chocolate Soufflé with Vanilla Cream—an elegant and indulgent dessert that combines the deep flavors of chocolate with warm spices and a creamy vanilla topping!

Balsamic Strawberry and Basil Sorbet

Ingredients:

- 4 cups (500g) fresh strawberries, hulled and halved
- 1 cup (200g) granulated sugar
- 1/4 cup (60ml) balsamic vinegar
- 1/2 cup (120ml) water
- 1 tablespoon freshly squeezed lemon juice

- 1/4 cup (10g) fresh basil leaves, finely chopped

Instructions:

1. **Prepare the Strawberry Mixture:**
    - **Blend Strawberries:** In a blender or food processor, combine the fresh strawberries and granulated sugar. Blend until smooth.
    - **Add Vinegar and Lemon Juice:** Add the balsamic vinegar and lemon juice to the blended strawberries and blend again until well combined.
2. **Chill the Mixture:**
    - **Refrigerate:** Transfer the strawberry mixture to a bowl and refrigerate for at least 1 hour, or until it is well chilled.
3. **Prepare the Sorbet Base:**
    - **Add Water:** Stir in the water into the chilled strawberry mixture.
    - **Mix in Basil:** Fold in the finely chopped basil leaves.
4. **Churn the Sorbet:**
    - **Ice Cream Maker:** Pour the sorbet mixture into an ice cream maker and churn according to the manufacturer's instructions until it reaches a soft-serve consistency.
    - **Alternative Method:** If you don't have an ice cream maker, pour the mixture into a shallow dish, place it in the freezer, and stir every 30 minutes until the sorbet is fully frozen and has a fluffy texture (about 4-6 hours).
5. **Freeze the Sorbet:**
    - **Final Freeze:** Transfer the churned sorbet to an airtight container and freeze for at least 2 hours to firm up.
6. **Serve:**
    - **Scoop and Garnish:** Scoop the sorbet into bowls or glasses. Garnish with additional basil leaves or a drizzle of balsamic vinegar if desired.

Tips:

- **Strawberries:** Use ripe, sweet strawberries for the best flavor. If strawberries are out of season, you can use frozen strawberries.
- **Balsamic Vinegar:** Choose a high-quality balsamic vinegar for a richer flavor. The vinegar adds a subtle tang that enhances the sweetness of the strawberries.
- **Chopping Basil:** Finely chop the basil to distribute the flavor evenly throughout the sorbet.

Enjoy your Balsamic Strawberry and Basil Sorbet—a sophisticated and refreshing treat that perfectly balances sweet, tangy, and herbal notes!

www.ingramcontent.com/pod-product-compliance
Lightning Source LLC
LaVergne TN
LVHW081558060526
838201LV00054B/1959